# THE
# CHILDREN'S
# SERMON

# THE
# CHILDREN'S
# SERMON

## Moments with GOD

### JANET S. HELME

CHALICE
PRESS

ST. LOUIS, MISSOURI

Visit Chalice Press on the World Wide Web at
www.chalicepress.com


10  9  8  7  6  5  4  3  2  1          10    11    12    13    14    15


EPUB: 978-08272-05239    EPDF: 978-08272-05246


**Library of Congress Cataloging-in-Publication Data**

Helme, Janet S.
The children's sermon : moments with God / by Janet S. Helme.
   p. cm.
ISBN 978-0-8272-0522-2
1. Preaching to children. 2. Children's sermons. I. Title.
BV4235.C4H45 2010
251'.53–dc22

                                                           2010008579


Printed in United States of America

# Contents

Introduction                                              1

1  Why a Children's Sermon?                               5

2  How Well Do You Know Your Audience?                    9

3  How Do You Craft the Children's Sermon?              16

4  What about the People in the Pews?                   23

5  What Are the Vital Tools for the Journey?            27

6  What Are Some Helpful Insights for the Journey?      31

7  Sample Children's Sermons, Lectionary Year B         38

    Advent 1                                     38

    Advent 2                                     45

    Epiphany 2                                   52

    Lent 1                                       58

    Lent 3                                       62

    Palm Sunday                                  67

8  Sample Children's Sermons, Lectionary Year C         73

    Lent 5                                       73

    Easter 2                                     80

    Easter 4                                     87

    Easter 6                                     91

    Proper 5                                     96

    Proper 19                                   101

9  Sample Children's Sermons, Lectionary Year A          107

    Advent 3                                              107

    Epiphany                                             115

    Lent 1                                               123

    Lent 3                                               128

    Easter                                               132

    Easter 5                                             136

Appendix A: Additional Ways to Include Children in the     143
    Worshiping Community

Appendix B: Recommended Books                             148

Appendix C: Scriptures Used                              152

# Introduction

After she had read the morning's scripture, the minister closed the Bible and said, in a friendly voice, "I invite the children to come forward now for the Children's Moment."

As the organist began to play a quiet interlude, I settled comfortably in my pew, looking forward to this "moment'" with the children. The minister for today was a person whom I admired very much. She enjoyed a lot of respect for the kinds of ministries she had led. I knew her personally as a woman of compassion, gentle humor, quick intelligence, and as a friend. She was an excellent preacher.

Holding a paper bag, she asked, "What do you think I have in this bag?" Various children offered suggestions: "your lunch," "a treat for us," "a surprise."

"No," she said with a grin. "I have a monkey in my bag."

By this time, all of the children's eyes watched her every move, waiting to see the monkey in her bag. Carefully showing the bag to the first child (who just happened to be a very outspoken little boy), the minister asked him, "See my monkey?" To which the little boy replied, "That's no monkey! That's just a mirror!"

At this loud declaration, the congregation began to chuckle and to laugh. Each child got the chance to see the "monkey in the bag," as the minister carried the bag past each of the eighteen children who sat on the steps of the chancel that morning. Several of the children repeated the first boy's objection, and some, with much enthusiasm, got into the game as they tried to outdo each other. "Hey, where's your monkey?" and "Watch out for the monkey in the bag!"

• • • • • • • •

Months later, I have no idea how the minister tied the "monkey in the bag" to the particular scripture she had read. Nor do I remember the point she was trying to make with this bag and mirror. But that Children's Moment raised one of the concerns I have had with many of the Children's Moments, or Children's Sermons, or Children's Time (however they are named) that I have heard in numerous churches. This concern centers on the inappropriate use of "object lessons," keeping in mind the median age of the children in most groups. Another problem is the way in which ministers appear to posture and parade to provide amusing entertainment for the congregation. Almost as an afterthought, they try to tell a story or make a point with the children.

• • • • • • • •

My educational background in child development and elementary education, plus years of teaching in public schools and private music lessons in my home, have helped to heighten my awareness of children, their comprehension levels, and their needs. As a longtime writer of children's church school curriculum materials, I appreciate my editors who have enhanced my awareness. Twenty-plus years in pastoral ministry have brought me face-to-face with lots of children with differing characteristics, needs, and desires. What a blessing this has been, to always be around children! Even more importantly, however, I feel much love and respect for every child. Each child is a special gift from God.

All these experiences and feelings made me realize I needed to share my concerns, thoughts, ideas, and learnings in a simple format so that other ministers, teachers, and child educators might have access to another way to work with children in the worshiping community of the church.

I have developed this book with the following seven objectives in mind:

1. to look closely at the purpose for the Children's Sermon
2. to examine just who the audience is, that is, their ages, their learning styles, and the ways in which they best understand the major themes of the Bible
3. to learn how to craft a good Children's Sermon, using the available lectionary scriptures and some other basics
4. to be aware of the congregation sitting "out there" as onlookers and of how to include and educate them in the Children's Sermon
5. to become aware of the various "tools of the trade" for doing Children's Sermons
6. to share some insights I have learned and used over the past twenty years in my ministry with children
7. to give some examples, step-by-step, for Children's Sermons to be used with Years A, B, and C of the Revised Common Lectionary.

• • • • • • • •

I have included Bible references throughout this book. We are a people of God. It is important to know why we do the things the way we do them. For me, our scriptures provide both a logical and theological beginning point. We can learn much by looking to the scriptures–particularly the teachings of Jesus, who both loved and respected the children in his midst.

May God bless you richly in the reading and the using of this book in whatever ways God guides you!

# CHAPTER 1

# Why a Children's Sermon?

*At that time the disciples came to Jesus and asked, "Who is the greatest in the kingdom of heaven?" He called a child, whom he put among them, and said, "Truly I tell you, unless you change and become like children, you will never enter the kingdom of heaven. Whoever becomes humble like this child is the greatest in the kingdom of heaven. Whoever welcomes one such child in my name welcomes me." (Mt. 18:1–5)*

One reason that we take the time, spend the energy, and provide the very best in a Children's Sermon is that we want to welcome children into our worship service. Children are important in the kingdom of God, as evidenced in the scripture passage above. Jesus told his disciples that those who welcome children in his name also welcome Jesus. We need to take care of the children in our midst and let them know they are a vital part of the worshiping community of faith.

Too often we have excluded our children from being a vital part of the worship service. We talk down to them, talk over their heads, try to "shush" and remove them if they get too noisy, or we pretend they do not exist. As an example, think about people exiting the sanctuary. How many times have you seen the minister actually bend down to a child's level, shake the child's hand, and talk with that child? Or is it more customary to see the minister shake the hands of the child's parents and, often, ignore the child?

Making children a vital part of the worship service does not mean that all children need to stay in the worship service during the entire sixty to seventy-five minutes. However, when they are in the worship service, we need to be very intentional about including them in some special ways. The Children's Sermon is just one way in which that inclusion can be effected. You will find examples of other ways to include children in the worshiping community in appendix A at the end of this book. However, the Children's Sermon–the topic of this book–is the beginning point for inclusion of children in worship.

• • • • • • • •

> You shall love the LORD your God with all your heart, and with all your soul, and with all your might. Keep these words that I am commanding you today in your heart. Recite them to your children and talk about them when you are at home and when you are away, when you lie down and when you rise. Bind them as a sign on your hand, fix them as an emblem on your forehead, and write them on the doorposts of your house and on your gates. (Deut. 6:5–9)

Another important reason for including a Children's Sermon is so that children begin to learn and recognize some of the important stories and concepts in the Bible. The Bible is an adult book. In fact, adults cannot begin to understand many stories in the Bible! Those are not the stories we want to use when we develop the Children's Sermon. This can, of course, be tricky if you are the person responsible for the Children's Sermon and another church leader chooses the scripture. You will find some helps with this in chapter 3, "How Do We Craft the Good Children's Sermon?" Suffice it to say that even in a long and convoluted text, we can usually find at least one phrase that can be used as a basis for the Children's Sermon. If not, then we build our children's presentation on a concept that comes out of that text, if at all possible. You will see examples of this also in chapters 3, and 7–9.

• • • • • • • •

> This is the covenant that I will make with the house of Israel
>     after those days, says the Lord.
> I will put my laws in their minds,
>     and write them on their hearts,
> and I will be their God,
>     and they shall be my people.
> And they shall not teach one another
>     or say to each other, "Know the Lord,"
> for they shall all know me,
>     from the least of them to the greatest. (Heb. 8:10–11)

A third important reason for including a Children's Sermon in the weekly worship service is to encourage children that scripture can "speak" to them today. If children learn at an early age to trust their parents, God, their Christian heritage through Jesus Christ and the Church, and what they learn from scripture, we have gone a long way in helping them to "write the scriptures" on their hearts. Of course, to have the scriptures written on their hearts, they must hear the scriptures.

Hear a note of caution. Many passages (over which biblical "authorities" have argued vehemently for years) must always remain a mystery in this lifetime. We do not introduce these scriptures to children at a young age. However, we can definitely introduce themes that children *can* understand, such as God is love; God loves me; God wants me to love others; and so on. Some of these themes are named and discussed in chapter 2, "How Well Do You Know Your Audience?"

A fourth important reason for including a weekly Children's Sermon is that it provides a wonderful opportunity to develop the prayer life of children. At the conclusion of the time with children, I always have them fold their hands, bow their heads, and repeat after me a very simple prayer, such as:

*"Thank you, God, for your love.*
*Help us to learn to love others*
*as you love us.*
*In Jesus' name we pray, Amen."*

This may be the only time that children engage in corporate prayer (or even in prayer of any kind), depending on your congregation and families. Children (and adults!) can learn from this brief prayer time that they do not have to use fancy words and that their prayers can be tied in directly to what they have just been hearing, learning, seeing, smelling, or touching.

The fifth and perhaps most important reason for including a weekly Children's Sermon is that we are, very intentionally, providing "moments with God" for the children in our churches.

A number of years ago while attending a ministers' spiritual retreat in Ohio, I heard the Reverend Peter Morgan say that the most important task of preachers is to "usher the people into the presence of God."

I believe that the most important task of those who provide the Children's Sermon each Sunday is to very intentionally guide our children into "moments with God"–moments when they glimpse the presence of God in their midst.

Last, however, I must include a caution. Over many years I have observed with anguish (but I hope have never intentionally employed during my children's sermons) how children are mistreated during this time.

Children should never, ever be used as entertainment for the congregation! They are not to be the butt of any joke or be used to make the congregation laugh. I have seen ordained ministers squirt water on unsuspecting children, ask them to do a task that they could not possibly do, or try to answer a question for which their answers could only appear silly–all in the name and context of the Children's Sermon.

The Children's Sermon can, definitely, have humor–but not at the expense of the children. Never at the expense of the children or of their feelings. What better way to turn children against the Church, God, and organized religion than to humiliate and/or embarrass them in front of the entire congregation?

I am always reminded of Jesus' admonition about our care of the "little ones" in our midst: "If any of you put a stumbling block before one of these little ones who believe in me, it would be better for you if a great millstone were fastened around your neck and you were drowned in the depth of the sea" (Mt. 18:6).

While this passage might indeed be referring to the new or young disciples in faith, I have always placed it on my heart as the care I must give as I work with and relate to the children who surround me wherever I am.

Seminary professors tell their students in preaching classes that every minute of a preached sermon should require one hour of preparation time. I would suggest that every minute of the Children's Sermon should include at least thirty minutes of solid preparation time. In other words, a four–minute Children's Sermon would require at least two hours of preparation. Not too much, in my estimation, for those whom Jesus named as "the greatest in the kingdom of heaven" (Mt. 18:1–2).

# CHAPTER 2

# How Well Do You Know Your Audience?

*For though I am free with respect to all, I have made myself
a slave to all, so that I might win more of them. To the Jews I
became as a Jew, in order to win Jews. To those under the law I
became as one under the law (though I myself am not under the
law) so that I might win those under the law. To those outside the
law I became as one outside the law (though I am not free from
God's law but am under Christ's law) so that I might win those
outside the law. To the weak I became weak, so that I might win
the weak. I have become all things to all people, that I might by
all means save some. I do it all for the sake of the gospel, so that I
may share in its blessings. (1 Cor. 9:19–23)*

The apostle Paul, the greatest missionary of Christianity, could
attribute part of his enormous success to the fact that he knew his
audience. Not only did he know them, but he also tried to present
the Gospel in ways that they could and would understand. William
Barclay, twentieth-century Scottish New Testament interpreter and
author, described Paul's method like this: "Finally, Paul speaks about
the method of his ministry, which was to become all things to all men.
This is not a case of being hypocritically one thing to one man and
another to another. It is a matter in the modern phrase, of being able
to get alongside anyone. The man who can never see anything but his
own point of view and who never makes any attempt to understand
the mind and heart of others, will never make a pastor or an evangelist
or even a friend."[1]

[1]William Barclay, *The Letter to the Corinthians,* rev. ed., The Daily Study Bible
Series (Philadelphia: The Westminster Press, 1977) 83.

I would add that neither can we hope to bring our children to God during the Children's Sermon unless we get to know them, trying to put ourselves in their shoes as they listen to us tell them something important about their church, God, Jesus, or themselves. If we hope to provide them a time and place to spend moments with God, we must know who they are, how they learn, and what their concerns and joys are.

The following list of questions is a beginning to learning more about the children who come to us each Sunday, eagerly and expectantly giving us their attention for several moments during the worship service:

- What are some differences among the children in the group?
- How do children learn in the worship service setting?
- What can we do to include children's various learning styles during the Children's Sermon?
- How can we, as leader or minister, get to know our children better?
- What are the major themes of scripture, and how do children understand them?

· · · · · · · ·

## What Are Some Differences among the Children in the Group?

Some notable differences among young children include differences of age, mental and physical growth/ability, emotional and spiritual levels, and differences in family relationships and support.

### Age

Perhaps the easiest difference to ascertain is the age of children. What is the usual age span of the children who come forward for the Children's Sermon? In which age group are the most children? Teachers, parents, and the associate minister and/or Christian education director can probably provide a list of the ages of all the children. I have found an index file card system helpful as I list each child's name, birth date, and other characteristics about him or her.

### Mental

What kinds of mental differences do you see in the children? Are they alert and able to follow your stories? Do they seem to be "with you" when you ask a question? Do you have any children who have mental challenges and special needs? If so, to whom can you speak/ listen to learn more about ways to accommodate these children with special mental challenges?

### Physical

Do you have a wide variance in the sizes of the children? What does this mean as far as where the children sit? Can the smaller children make eye contact with you? Do the larger children seem self-conscious because of their size? What can you do to make each of these children feel comfortable with the physical situation of the Children's Sermon?

### Emotional

Do some children in your group cry or cause other kinds of disturbances? What are some ways to deal with these differences? Could you recruit an adult to sit beside that particular child? Would talking with the parents to work on a solution be helpful? Could a parent accompany the child to the Children's Sermon?

As an example of emotional problems, I once had a child who seemed to be very intelligent. Both her Sunday school teacher and the teachers for the extended session had commented to me on her intellectual capabilities. However, this child had a definite emotional disability. If things didn't go her way—in almost every respect—she would cry, have a tantrum, or stomp out of the sanctuary. Only later did I learn that she suffered from a particular syndrome and needed to be kept on special medications faithfully so that this behavior was at a minimum. Having this knowledge gave me better ways to work with her during the Children's Sermon.

### Spiritual

Children will, of course, be at different spiritual levels and have varying religious understandings. Some will have a very basic understanding of God, the Church, religion, Jesus, worship, and so on. Others will have spent enough time in church to have a much greater understanding. This is an excellent opportunity for the more advanced spiritual children to help provide some great learning for the rest of the children.

### Relational

Knowing about a child's family and other relationships can also help you know that child better. Do you know anything about the parent or parents? Are there other siblings (younger and/or older)? Does the child live with extended family in the home? Does the child have other relatives in your church?

As you discover various characteristics, keep adding them to your index cards. Use these file cards, then, as a weekly/ monthly reminder to keep you up-to-date and knowledgeable about the children in your church. As you plan the Children's Sermon, you will (like the senior minister crafts sermons to the needs of the congregation) be able to craft them with your particular audience in mind.

### How Do Children Learn?

Children, just like adults, learn by use of the five senses and other methods. I have listed these, not in order of the most common way of learning, but by the teaching method most persons use in presenting the Children's Sermon.

**Children learn by listening:** This may be the least effective way for children to learn, even though we continue to use it again and again. Especially for children who have difficulty sitting still and paying attention, talking, by itself, is not the most effective way to present a Children's Sermon.

**Children learn by seeing:** Adding some kind of visual aid can enhance the Children's Sermon greatly. The visual aid can be as simple as a colorful picture, a poster, or an object, such as a ceramic bowl.

**Children learn by touching:** How much more a child can learn if, in addition to hearing and seeing, they are able to touch something– dipping a finger into a bowl of water, stroking a piece of velvet fabric, feeling the hardness of a brick or the smoothness of a new baseball bat.

**Children learn by smelling:** Who can resist the smell of a loaf of freshly baked bread or the whiff of a rose? Smelling is a sense that is always ready, but so seldom used. Including smells in the Children's Sermon provides a new, unique experience.

**Children learn by tasting:** We should never forget that tasting can be absolutely sublime, especially if it is an enticement such as a piece of cookie, or fruit, or a crunchy pretzel.

**Children learn by experiencing:** This one, sometimes, is the most difficult to do in the short time allowance you have. However, even watching one child experience something can be a time of learning for the entire group of children.

**Children learn best by a combination of the above methods:** Especially is it important to vary the methods of presentation so that children keep their sense of excitement as they come forward for the Children's Sermon, never knowing exactly what they will hear, see, touch, smell, taste, or experience. These "moments with God" need to be, for them, one of the most important parts of the Sunday worship experience.

### Some Additional Ways to Know Your Audience

To get better acquainted with the children in your church, you could also try some or all of the following:

- Visit their Sunday school classes
- Talk with the teachers of their classes
- Volunteer to substitute in their Sunday school classes
- Visit their homes
- Invite specific children and parents to visit with you after church or during another activity that occurs in the church setting. *As a word of caution,* always be certain that one or more parents is involved in this setting. Never meet with a child by yourself.

### An Example of an Index Card with Specific Information

**NAME:** Daisy Johnson
**AGE:** 4 years old
**BIRTHDAY:** July 16, 2003
**PARENTS:** Linda Johnson (parents divorced; Linda and Daisy live with L's parents)
**PHONE:** 926–5000
**ADDRESS:** 123 Lake Drive
**COMMENTS:** Daisy is well-developed physically and mentally, very alert. Seems to have had a good foundation of faith from her family. Timid about speaking in front of a crowd, but she can always be heard when the children pray our prayer together.
Visited the family twice, impressed with their genuine hospitality toward me. Both grandparents and mother seem to show a lot of love to Daisy.

## What Are the Major Themes of Scripture, and How Do Children Understand Them?

While writing church school and vacation Bible school curricula, I learned that particular themes continue to repeat themselves in the Bible.

One interdenominational group identified nine major themes in the Bible. They then interpreted these themes in language that young children, primary children, and junior children can understand. Looking for these nine themes can be very helpful when we begin to prepare the Children's Sermon for any given Sunday.

Each of the themes, of course, is understood just a little differently as children get older, but I have always tried to see the theme in the simplest terms. That way, the younger children in the group–as well as the older children–have a much better chance of relating to what I am trying to tell, explain, or teach.[2]

The nine major themes and the words that the youngest children, ages 2–5, can understand are:

1. *Creation*–God made me; God made everything.
2. *God's Self-Revelation*–God is good; God loves me; Jesus loves us.
3. *Sin*–Doing wrong disappoints God; doing wrong hurts me; doing wrong hurts others.
4. *Judgment*–What we do really does matter; we live with the outcomes of our choices; God makes us able to choose.
5. *Redemption*–God loves me all the time; God loves me even when I do wrong; God loves me when I'm good and when I'm not good.
6. *People of God*–I belong to God's family; I am a part of the Church;
7. *Providence*–God plans for a good world; God helps us.
8. *Hope*–God always keeps God's promises; God will always take care of me; God is always with me.
9. *Faith-Response*–Thank you, God; I love you, God; Help me; I'll help you; I'm happy.

Why do we need to know these themes? What is their significance as we craft the Children's Sermon? This can best be explained and

---

[2]"Biblical Themes in Primary Terms," *Primary Teacher's Resource Guide,* Growing with the Bible (Crawfordsville, Ind.: Micheal Bergamo, 1982), 4.

illustrated as we work through a scripture to develop a good Children's Sermon, which we shall do in chapter 3. However, if you begin to get familiar with these themes and how children understand them, you will find it much easier to relate many of the Bible's stories and teachings to the children's level of understanding.

# How Do You Craft the Children's Sermon?

*"Again, the kingdom of heaven is like a merchant in search of fine pearls; on finding one pearl of great value, he went and sold all that he had and bought it." (Mt. 13:45–46)*

Jesus told the above parable to remind his followers that anything of worth requires effort on their part. As you think about and plan for each week's Children's Sermon, be assured that a good one will take time, planning, and some special skills, which you can learn.

### It All Begins with Prayer and Silence

The most important thing we can do, as we begin crafting a Children's Sermon, is to begin in prayer. If you are not in the habit of daily prayer, I would suggest that you start with even a very simple prayer:

*I ask, God, that you guide my thoughts, my words, and my actions as I begin my work on the Children's Sermon for next Sunday. Help me see the very best way in which I can present the scripture to this group of children. I want them to feel your presence with them. I want them to be present to you. Fill me with your Holy Spirit. In the name of Jesus, Amen.*

A time of silence is a necessary part of this kind of focused prayer. The silence enables God to place ideas and direction into our minds. Sometimes I've experienced these kinds of God-helps within a couple of hours of my prayer for guidance. At other times they may not appear until several days later.

I find it helpful to relax, lean back against my chair, placing both feet on the floor, and my hands in my lap, palms up. Trying to keep outer (and inner) distractions at a minimum, I strive to spend ten to twenty minutes in quiet listening time after I've prayed for God's guidance. I know, from both personal experience and talking with others, that God provides faithful guidance to us whenever we take the time to ask and to listen.

As you get more used to this kind of prayer (asking God's guidance in each step of the process), you may begin to feel very comfortable lifting up in prayer several times a week your need for help. I am convinced that God wants nothing more than to be a vital part of our everyday existence—especially in an area as important as bringing our children closer to God.

## Selecting and Studying the Scripture

The next step in crafting the Children's Sermon is selection of a scripture. You may not get to choose your own scripture. This is especially true if you are not the person preaching that day.

For purposes of this book, we shall use the Revised Common Lectionary scriptures. You may already know that the lectionary includes four scriptures for every Sunday in the year:

- one scripture from the Hebrew Bible (our Old Testament)
- one scripture from the psalms
- one scripture from the gospels
- one scripture from the epistles, or letters, usually in the New Testament

The lectionary is on a three-year rotating cycle listed as A, B, and C. I have chosen scriptures for several from each of the three years for this particular book (see chapters 7–9 for samples from each year).

For this chapter we shall look at the lectionary scriptures for the first Sunday in Advent, Year A. Advent is the season that begins the fourth Sunday before Christmas Day. In most churches that use the lectionary Advent will be celebrated on each of those four Sundays before Christmas Day. Because Advent is the time in the Church calendar when people try to experience and proclaim the hope in which ancient Israel waited and longed for the promised Messiah, the chosen scriptures may appear somewhat somber. This does not mean, however, that the Children's Sermon has to be somber, as you will see in the examples.

Sometimes, at first glance, I have read the four scriptures for a particular Sunday and asked myself, "How can I ever find an appropriate topic from these scriptures?"

This is what I hope to help clarify as we look at Advent 1, Year A.

The four scripture selections are

- Isaiah 2:1–5
- Psalm 122
- Romans 13:11–14
- Matthew 24:36–44

I offer the following steps for doing the initial preparation, using the Isaiah 2 scripture. (In chapters 7–9 I will go into more detail as to why I would choose one scripture over another.) This method can, of course, be used with any of the above scriptures.

### 1. Read the Scripture

You will need one or two good translations of the Bible, a notepad or several index cards, and pencil and/or pen.

Find a quiet place—without distractions—so that you can read the scripture. Normally I use the *New Revised Standard Version,* which is a very accurate translation from the original languages (Hebrew and Greek) into English.

Often, I also read from *The Good News Bible,* also known as *Today's English Version.* This Bible is probably the best conceptual translation from the original languages. That is, the concepts in the original setting are translated into concepts in our times that are most similar and meaningful to us. In addition, if you plan to read a verse or two to them, children will better understand *The Good News Bible/Today's English Version.*

I use the following four steps in my scripture reading:

- Read the scripture  silently to yourself.
- Reread the scripture, aloud, slowly, thinking about each word you are reading.
- Now read the scripture a third time, but this time offer it up as a prayer to God as though you are talking with God about this important message from the Bible.
- On the notepad or index cards, write down any questions or thoughts you have about this scripture—things you don't understand, some "Aha!" moments where something became

very clear to you, anything you think the children would relate to well.

### 2. Study One or Two Good Resources for Understanding the Scripture

My two favorite, easy-to-understand resources for lectionary scriptures are:

*Preaching the Revised Common Lectionary* by Abingdon Press, which can be purchased online or at any Cokesbury store. These are a series of books grouped by seasons (Advent, Pentecost, Lent, Easter, etc.) for each of the three cycles: A, B, and C. Perhaps your church library or your pastor has copies you could borrow.

The *Daily Study Bible Series Commentaries: Old Testament and New Testament.* The commentaries for the New Testament were written by William Barclay in the 1950s and 1960s and still are some of the best that have been written. They provide much information on what was happening at the time of the writing of the scripture, why it was written, to whom and by whom, etc. Barclay died before he could write the commentaries for the books of the Old Testament, but fortunately other scholars have completed the series. Again, church libraries, ministers, and even some public and religious libraries (seminaries, denominational/Catholic colleges) have these commentaries in their collections.

The Holman Old Testament and New Testament Commentaries edited by Max Anders and the Tyndale Old Testament and New Testament Commentaries are also good for laity. A step advanced from these are the New Interpreter's Bible.

As you read about the particular sections of scripture in the above resources, use your written notes from your reading of the scripture (see the last bullet under Step 1 above), and write what you learn from these biblical resources. This can help you as you prepare the words you may be saying to the children during the Children's Sermon.

### 3. Identify the Major Themes in the Scripture, Using the Nine Major Themes Listed in Chapter 2

With Isaiah 2:1–5, these are the themes I identified:

- Hope–v. 2
- Faith-Response–v. 3, v. 4 b, c, d, and v. 5
- Judgment–v. 4
- Providence–vv. 2–5

### 4. Consider the Different Approaches to this Scripture and the Children's Sermon

You can introduce the Children's Sermon in many ways. For this particular scripture, I considered the following:

- Verse and Graphic (listening and visual senses)
- Touch (kinesthetic)
- Experiential (doing and discussing)

I chose the first approach (others will be defined and illustrated in Chapters 7–9).

### 5. Make a Brief Outline of What You Plan to Say and Do and What You Need

I typically use a 5 x 8" index card as I outline my thoughts. I use that card when I gather with the children on Sunday morning, having made changes or corrections. I carry my large Bible with me, placing the index card in the page with the chosen scripture passage.

## A Sample Children's Sermon Using a Verse and Graphic Approach

### Materials Needed

- a large picture of your church on a poster, with Isaiah 2:2–3 written below the picture of your church
- a worship bulletin or other tangible, nonbreakable item from your worship service
- a handout for each child (see chapter 5 for specific information on handouts)

### Theme Used: Faith-Response (Isaiah 2:2–3)

### Steps of the Children's Sermon

1. Invite the children forward and greet them with "Good morning, I'm happy to see you today!" (Or something similar, letting them know you're glad they are here.)
2. Show the children the picture of your church.
3. Point out the Isaiah scripture below the church. Read the words to them. Explain that in this Bible verse, God's prophet Isaiah is making a promise to the Hebrew people, who are going through bad times. Isaiah tells them that good days are ahead. One day many people will go to the temple so that they can learn about

God. They will know what God wants them to do. God will teach them how to live godly lives.

### Questions: Ask the children the following questions

- How do you and I learn to live godly lives?
- Who or what helps us with this?

### Affirmation and Question from You, the Leader

"Yes, we have different ways to learn about what God wants us to do. Our parents and other family members teach us. We can read the Bible or listen to Bible stories that others read to us. Some of these Bible stories tell us about Jesus, and he shows us how to live in godly ways. Also, we come to Sunday school and church, where our Sunday school teachers and our ministers teach us. How blessed we are to have all these different ways to learn about God and about Jesus!"

### Prayer: Ask the children to bow their heads and pray after you, a simple prayer

*Thank you, God, for loving us.*
*Thank you for the Bible,*
*which tells us about Jesus.*
*Thank you for our church*
*and our teachers.*
*In Jesus' name, Amen.*

### The Handout

On the next page is a sample handout for a different scripture. I will discuss the importance of handouts in chapter 5, "What Are the Vital Tools for the Journey?"

Say to the children: "Here is your handout for today. I'd like you to take it home with you and place it where it will be a reminder of what we talked about today. We are blessed that we can come to Sunday school and church to learn more about God. Our teachers and minister help us learn how to live as God wants us to live."

This Children's Sermon should take about four minutes from start to finish. I have often found it helpful for the persons who will be taking the children to Children's Worship or Children's Church (if you provide this) to sit near the front so that they can distribute the handouts that I provide for the children to take home each Sunday. Or recruit a parent or deacon to help with this so that the children can receive their handouts in a timely manner.

"My soul magnifies the Lord, and my spirit rejoices in God,"

Luke 1:46-55
(Mo, day, yr)

# CHAPTER 4

# What about the People in the Pews?

*[Jesus] also said, "With what can we compare the kingdom of God, or what parable will we use for it? It is like a mustard seed, which, when sown upon the ground, is the smallest of all the seeds on earth; yet when it is sown it grows up and becomes the greatest of all shrubs, and puts forth large branches, so that the birds of the air can make nests in its shade." ( Mk. 4:30–32)*

Jesus was trying to make the point that small beginnings are not necessarily a forecast of how something will ultimately end. Often the efforts we make, and God's bountiful graces along the way, can produce amazing results!

This parable supports the point I am trying to make: the Children's Sermon is of utmost importance as a way to help children experience moments with God. The children may be small. The number of children may be small. The amount of time in the total worship experience may be small. But all of these can be brought to great proportions through our efforts, laced with God's bountiful blessings and graces.

The congregation also plays a major role in this event, and we, as leaders and crafters of the Children's Sermon, must help them identify and accept their role.

## The Roles of the Congregation in The Children's Sermon
### *Review of the Purposes of the Children's Sermon*

To look at the role of the congregation during the Children's Sermon, it is important that we review again the purposes of the Children's Sermon. This will help to clarify what role the congregation plays in this process. Beginning with the most important, those purposes are as follow:

- to provide the children moments with God in which they get to know God better and to feel God's presence among them
- to welcome children into the worshiping community during the worship service
- to assist the children in learning and recognizing some of the important stories and concepts in the Bible
- to help children know that the scriptures in our Bible can have meaning for their lives
- to assist the children in developing a prayer life with God.

The congregation (members, frequent visitors, and first-time visitors) have various roles in which they participate during the Children's Sermon:

- Good listeners. The assembled congregation, the "people in the pews," are ones who can listen carefully to what the leader is sharing with the children during this time. For this to happen, the leader must have adequate amplification, especially because as our congregations get older, we have many more persons who are hearing impaired. Making it easier for people to listen carefully provides them with the opportunity to learn what the children are being taught and perhaps to engage one of the children in conversation after the service about what they have learned.
- Ones who overhear a sacred moment. This time with the children during the Children's Sermon is to be a time to provide "moments with God." It is every bit as important as the rest of the worship service. This can easily be a time when we experience a sacred moment, a time that is profound in its connection to God and in God's connection to us. If the congregation is listening attentively, they may also get to experience this sacred moment. It can possibly be a time that may change a person's life, an epiphany, an "Aha!" moment.
- Prayer mentors. Providing a prayer mentor for each of the babies, children, and youth in a congregation is an especially powerful way to strengthen your congregation. (See appendix A for suggestions on ways to do this). If you are doing this already, then the mentors of these particular children can be lifting them in prayer, very intentionally, during the Children's

Sermon. In addition, all members of the congregation can be praying for the children who are gathered, those who might be absent on a particular morning, and the leader of the Children's Sermon.

• Participants (by invitation). Sometimes the Children's Sermon will need congregational participation. When this occurs (and you can see some examples in chapters 7–9), you as the leader will need to alert the congregation and be very specific about what they are to do.

### *Things for the Congregation to Avoid*

I have found some behaviors and reactions to be detrimental to the purposes of and the reasons for the Children's Sermon:

1. laughter at the children's responses
2. clapping hands for the children's "performance"
3. taking pictures during the Children's Sermon or related events

How do we let the congregation know about these behaviors and reactions that do not necessarily contribute to helping our children to grow in godly ways? Some of the ideas listed below, in "Communication Is a Must," may be helpful to get you started on ways you can educate your congregation about being the most helpful they can be during the Children's Sermon.

### *Communication Is a Must*

To help educate the congregation so they can assist in the nurturing of our children in the way they should grow, we must find ways to communicate faithfully with them. Here are some of the helpful ways I have found to do this:

• newsletter articles
• bulletin inserts
• pamphlets of explanation that remain in the hymnal racks
• an occasional display of information in a narthex, foyer, or gathering place
• short presentations to the church board or women's/men's groups
• short visits to the various adult Sunday school classes
• individual conversations with leaders in the congregation
• preaching on the topic of children; this would be especially effective during the month of October and/or on Children's Sabbath, usually the third Sunday of October.

## Samples of Communication Tools

### Newsletter Article

Have you ever wondered, "Why do we have a Children's Sermon each Sunday? What's the point?" We as a church have lots of reasons for taking this time in our weekly worship service. Here are just two:

1. Children feel welcomed when they are included in some way in our worship service. Suddenly it means more to them. They have a place in our worship.
2. Children can begin to recognize stories from our Bible, and this is exciting! These stories will be "written on their hearts" just as God intended them to be.

### Bulletin Insert

Your church staff invites you to be good listeners during the Children's Sermon every Sunday. This emphasizes to our children that you care about them and about what they are learning in this special time. You may learn something new too!

CHAPTER 5

# What Are the Vital Tools for the Journey?

*Keep these words that I am commanding you today in your heart. Recite them to your children and talk about them when you are at home and when you are away, when you lie down and when you rise. Bind them as a sign on your hand, fix them as an emblem on your forehead, and write them on the doorposts of your house and on your gates. (Deut. 6:6–9)*

Some things in life we need to remember. Such things can make a difference to us in the ways we view our past, live in the present, and look toward the future. Moses knew this. The Jewish people knew this. Moses told them in the Shema Prayer that they must always remember that "the LORD is our God, the LORD alone. You shall love the LORD your God with all your heart, and with all your soul, and with all your might" (Deut. 6:4–5). Then Moses gave them some specific examples of what they needed to do to remember these words. These actions were vital to their living as the people of God.

They were to recite these words, to know them by memory. As a family, they needed to talk about the Shema, both in their homes and in their travels. Morning and evening rituals were to be built around these words, describing who God was and is. The Shema must be *visible* on their hands, on their foreheads, and on the doorposts and gates of their homes.

## The Available Tools

Some of the tools vital for creating a good Children's Sermon are also tools that can help the children remember what they have seen, touched, heard, and, we hope, learned.

27

· · · · · · ·

### The Visual

Have you heard the adage "a picture is worth a thousand words"? Often this is true, especially when we work with children. By seeing one picture we can often take in, at a glance, what a story is describing. Using visuals proves helpful when I'm trying to make a point or telling a story during the Children's Sermon.

Where do I get my visuals? Many sources are available: art books, especially Christian art books; *Imaging the Word: An Arts and Lectionary Resource,* volumes 1, 2, and 3; and the art piece, *Behold,* of the curriculum series, Seasons of the Spirit. Check appendix B for more information.

Whenever churches I've served have gotten rid of old curriculum materials, I have usually taken the time to search through the various pieces, collecting pictures. Then I categorize the pictures into a picture file under subject headings, such as "Bible stories," "scenery," "people," "animals," "buildings," etc. I also make a habit of visiting the public library, which is a good place to find wonderful pictures in the children's picture book section. Sometimes I find a book that I know I will use over and over again, so I purchase it.

I have also bought special children's books from church publishing companies. I look at the seasonal flyers that these religious publishers send out. Whenever possible, I visit secular book stores so I can browse through the children's section. (See a listing of suggested books in appendix B.)

Sometimes I create an art piece on my computer with art software. You will find additional information about the excellent graphics program I use under the next section, "The Handout."

Some of the other sources I have used for visuals include magazines, posters, greeting cards, calendars, and photographs. Once you begin thinking about visuals, you will begin to see possibilities all around you!

### The Handout

This particular tool reminds me most of the Deuteronomy passage listed at the beginning of this chapter. I give each child a handout every time I lead the Children's Sermon. I often remind them to take this handout home, go over it with their families, and then place it in a spot where they will see it and remember what it means. This is a tangible reminder for them of what we have talked about and learned during their special time in the worship service. It also helps to get their family members involved with that week's particular lesson.

I create these very simple handouts, using Broderbund's The Print Shop Deluxe II and its postcard program (MS Publisher, Adobe's InDesign, and many other graphics programs are also available. Several Web sites feature classical and contemporary biblical art, though their restrictions on use vary, so read the site carefully). Using cardstock in my printer, I can make four postcards per page. Normally I have a portion of a scripture verse, a small graphic, and sometimes a question or a short prayer.

If you want a sample of an original handout, you may send a self-addressed, stamped envelope to Rev. Janet Helme, 6147 W Ave. J-5, Lancaster, CA 93536–7589. Here is an example:

This is the Day which the LORD has Made!

Palm Sunday (mo, day, year)

Parents and grandparents have shared with me some of the creative ways they have collected these handouts for their children. One grandmother was making scrapbooks of all the visuals her grandchildren were receiving every week. She planned to give them as a gift to each one for Christmas. Another grandmother had started a bulletin board display. Both of them said they talked with their grandchildren about what they were learning each week during the Children's Sermon.

A number of Internet sites offer free children's sermon helps. One particularly good site for color pages and puzzles is www.textweek.

com. This site shows lectionary materials for every week of the year. Each of the scriptures has its own page, including a section on the Children's Sermon. While this site is free, they do encourage and accept donations to keep the Web site operational.

•••••••

The two most important tools for the journey are the visual and the weekly handout. Of course, I usually have my Bible with me. Often I read a phrase or a verse from it. At other times it is just a visible object that the children get used to seeing. I remind the children in some way each week that what we are talking about and sharing comes from our Bible. In my present congregation, on Children's Sabbath (the third Sunday in October), we give all the children a new Bible. Even our babies! To learn more about Children's Sabbath (what and when it is, suggestions for how to celebrate it in your church), see www.childrensdefense.org or search for "children's sabbath" on your denominational Web site.

# CHAPTER SIX

# What Are Some Helpful Insights for the Journey?

*Then Jesus called the twelve together and gave them power and authority over all demons and to cure diseases, and he sent them out to proclaim the kingdom of God and to heal. He said to them, "Take nothing for your journey, no staff, nor bag, nor bread, nor money—not even an extra tunic. Whatever house you enter, stay there, and leave from there. Wherever they do not welcome you, as you are leaving that town shake the dust off your feet as a testimony against them." They departed and went through the villages, bringing the good news and curing diseases everywhere. (Lk. 9:1–6)*

Jesus knew that for his disciples to do their best on the mission to which they were called, they must be prepared. They needed to know what to take and what not to take for this mission. They needed to know where to stay and how to leave when it was time. They even needed to know how to exit a house or a town if the townspeople did not welcome them. Jesus gave them very specific instructions for all of this.

Paul also helped prepare others. Paul's first letter to Timothy, one of his protégés, sought to make Timothy the best minister of Jesus Christ that he could be. Paul's words of wisdom to Timothy have helped countless ministers through the ages learn good skills of preparation:

These are the things you must insist on and teach. Let no one despise your youth, but set the believers an example in speech and conduct, in love, in faith, in purity. Until I arrive, give attention to the public reading of scripture, to exhorting, to teaching. Do not neglect the gift that is in you, which was given to you through prophecy with the laying on of hands by the council of elders. Put these things into practice, devote yourself to them, so that all may see your progress. Pay close attention to yourself and to your teaching; continue in these things, for in doing this you will save both yourself and your hearers. (1 Tim. 4:11–16)

Paul knew Timothy might need some helpful advice to help him succeed in the special ministry Timothy had undertaken. Timothy was young, so Paul was also building up Timothy's self-concept when he told Timothy to "Let no one despise your youth." Timothy had many skills. He was venturing into new waters, but he could do so, knowing that God had definitely gifted him and called him into ministry. Paul told Timothy to remember the gift that was in him, "which was given to [him] through prophecy with the laying on of hands by the council of elders."

## Steps to Success in Your Ministry with Children

If you are reading and studying this book, you probably are either a senior minister with a special heart for children or have been called or anointed or chosen to work with the children's ministry in your church. You may be looking seriously to improve what you have been doing. You want to be as prepared as possible. Below I have listed seven ways to assist you in reaching your best level of preparedness:

1. Always pray before you begin this time of preparation.
2. Practice from your outline.
3. Listen to your speaking voice.
4. Concentrate on your facial features.
5. Remember to extend hospitality.
6. Recruit a 'live guinea pig' for feedback.
7. Enlist helpers where needed.

• • • • • • •

### *Pray before You Begin*

Always remember to pray when you are preparing yourself to do the Children's Sermon. God wants nothing more than for you to succeed in this very special and important ministry in your church. God wants those children to have a relationship with God. God wants to guide them throughout their lives. God wants the people in the pews to learn how important it is that children are brought into the presence of God. Perhaps God is hoping that some of your Children's Sermon will "rub off" on the adults!

One simple prayer is:

"God, I know how much you want to touch the lives of the children in our church. Please guide me as I prepare for their time with you. Let me have the patience to sit in silence—even if for only a few minutes—so that you might instill into my mind some thoughts and words that I might use. All this I do for your honor and glory, and in Jesus' name I pray, Amen."

### *Practice from Your Outline*

In chapter 3, "How Do We Craft the Children's Sermon?" I suggested using a 5 X 8" index card for a prop. You write down the date, the topic, what teaching materials you need , and the steps of your Children's Sermon. I usually write down a phrase to help me remember what I want to say to, or ask the children. I always do it in a little larger print so that I can read it at a quick glance.

Using this index card, go through your Children's Sermon from start to finish, more than once. See if it makes good sense to you. Use a stopwatch to time how long it lasts. Then ask yourself questions:

- Will my group of children understand what I am telling or asking them?
- Am I using the most effective presentation technique?
- What will they learn from this time together?
- What will be their new understanding of God, Jesus, the Holy Spirit, the congregation, or themselves?
- How will this message help to shape or change their lives?

If you cannot answer any of the above questions, you need to do some reshaping of your time with the children. Go back and review the information in chapters 2 and 3.

### *Listen to Your Speaking Voice*

One good way to listen to how your voice sounds is to record yourself, in your own home or private room, as you go through the Children's Sermon from start to finish. (This can also help with practicing from your outline. You may discover that you have forgotten to make an important point or transition. You may hear something you need to add or delete).

Do you speak too fast? Do you emphasize the wrong words? Are you saying too many "uhs" or using too many slang fillers, "you know," or "like . . ." Does your voice convey excitement, sincerity, and interest in the children?

A good check for how you are sounding in the actual worship service is to listen to a tape, if your church tapes services. Or have someone tape your portion of the service. Listen to these tapes from the perspective of yourself, and then from that of the children, and finally, that of the congregation (although, remember that they are just "overhearing" your Children's Sermon; it is not for them).

### Concentrate on Your Facial Features

Standing in front of a bathroom mirror (hopefully, when nobody else is around!), go through parts or all of the Children's Sermon. Check to see if your facial features are pleasant rather than frowning as you concentrate on something. Do you occasionally have a glimmer or a twinkle in your eyes, indicating that you are really enjoying what you are doing? Do you have an inviting demeanor?

If you are fortunate enough to have a camcorder, set it up and record yourself presenting a Children's Sermon. (Or perhaps your congregation makes a DVD of its services. If so, borrow one that has you on it.) As you view yourself, try to put yourself into the mind of a child. What would you find pleasing about yourself? What seems to be a little harsh? What could be improved to enhance your presentation?

### Remember to Extend Hospitality Always

We always need to practice hospitality in the church. We are God's ambassadors for everyone who walks through the church doors. Nowhere is it more important than with the children in the church. If parents and other relatives see how much their children are welcomed into and loved by the worshiping community, they will continue to bring them to you on a regular basis.

Hospitality is looking for ways to make the children feel accepted and wanted. Hospitality is extending God's love, through you, to them.

Hospitality is putting their needs above your own. Hospitality is behaving in such a way that the children can say to themselves, "This person really wants me to be here!"

Hospitality happens when we invite the children to come forward with an eagerness in our voice.

Hospitality is the way in which we greet the children, smile at them, and look at them throughout the Children's Sermon. An excellent resource book on hospitality is *The Gift of Hospitality: in the Church, in the Home, in All of Life* by Delia Halverson. (Check appendix B, Recommended Books).

### Recruit a Live "Guinea Pig"

To really check out how you are doing (and to get some hands-on experience at the same time), ask a young relative, a neighbor child, a friend's child, etc., to help you as you prepare to give a Children's Sermon by listening to you. Invite the parent(s) of the child. Their feedback will also be helpful and valuable to you. If you are on staff at a church, you might invite other staff or committee members who either have children or teach children. Explain the kinds of things they will be hearing and seeing, and the areas in which you would like some special feedback, i.e., "Do I look like I'm excited about what I'm sharing?"

When you are finished and ready to receive their comments, have an index card available so that you can jot down their comments. Even if you do not agree with a comment, go ahead and record it. It may come in handy at a later time. Always thank them for helping you (even though you may think they're off base).

### Enlist Helpers Where Needed

Sometimes even the best of God's people needs some extra help. One of my favorite Bible stories related to helpers is about Moses and how he worked so hard to help his Hebrew people. It got to be too much for him, but his father-in-law Jethro came to his rescue with a new plan:

> The next day Moses sat as judge for the people, while the people stood around him from morning until evening. When Moses' father-in-law saw all that he was doing for the people, he said, "What is this that you are doing for the people? Why do you sit alone, while all the people stand around you from morning until evening?" Moses said to his father-in-law, "Because the people come to me to inquire of God. When they have a dispute, they come to me and I decide between one person and another, and I make known to them the statutes and instructions of God." Moses' father-in-law said to him, "What you are doing is not good. You will surely wear yourself out, both you and these people

with you. For the task is too heavy for you; you cannot do it alone. Now listen to me. I will give you counsel, and God be with you! You should represent the people before God, and you should bring their cases before God; teach them the statutes and instructions and make known to them the way they are to go and the things they are to do. You should also look for able men among all the people, men who fear God, are trustworthy, and hate dishonest gain; set such men over them as officers over thousands, hundreds, fifties and tens. Let them sit as judges for the people at all times; let them bring every important case to you, but decide every minor case themselves. So it will be easier for you, and they will bear the burden with you. If you do this, and God so commands you, then you will be able to endure, and all these people will go to their home in peace." (Ex. 18:13–23)

Sometimes I am like the "former Moses," trying to do everything myself. I don't do this because I think I have all the answers. Rather, I get busy and don't get the tasks organized well enough ahead of time so that I can delegate some of the responsibilities. All of God's ministers, ordained and licensed or lay leaders, need good helpers.

One of the easiest helper tasks to assign (especially if you have more than eight to ten children who come forward for the Children's Sermon) is the responsibility of distributing your weekly handouts for the children. You can show the handout and explain it before you have the children pray with you. Then the helpers can pass out the handouts as children go back to their seats, or the children can follow the helpers out of the sanctuary for an extended session or Children's Worship, etc. This process helps the worship service to continue to flow smoothly into the next phase. It also ensures that the Children's Sermon does not extend beyond its time limit.

Another task would be for those times when you want to create a more tangible handout, such as a small paper or cardboard sheep for each child to take home as a reminder. If you have a sewing group or a women's group (or a women's/men's group of creative persons), they can be invaluable as you develop different kinds of simple handouts for the children. Use your congregation in creative ways to help this children's ministry be the very best it can be.

A third way to involve persons is to begin training them to learn how to present the Children's Sermon. There will be Sundays when you are unable to do this. It's always good to train others to be able to just step in, whenever necessary, and continue the good work you are doing.

Remember the story of Moses and his father-in-law, Jethro. Pray that God will lead you to the people who have the love, the desire, and gifts to share with the children in your church.

# CHAPTER 7

# Sample Children's Sermons, Lectionary Year B

## YEAR B, ADVENT 1

### A. Scriptures

Isaiah 64:1–9; Psalm 80:1–7, 17–19; Mark 13:24–37; 1 Corinthians 1:3–9

### B. Process of Selection

Read each scripture and write down possible verses to use with children.

### 1. Isaiah 64:1–9

1   O that you would tear open the heavens and come down,
     so that the mountains would quake at your presence—
2   as when fire kindles brushwood
     and the fire causes water to boil—
    to make your name known to your adversaries,
     so that the nations might tremble at your presence!
3   When you did awesome deeds that we did not expect,
     you came down, the mountains quaked at your presence.
4   From ages past no one has heard,
     no ear has perceived,
    no eye has seen any God besides you,
     who works for those who wait for him.
5   You meet those who gladly do right,
     those who remember you in your ways.
    But you were angry, and we sinned;
     because you hid yourself we transgressed.
6   We have all become like one who is unclean,
     and all our righteous deeds are like a filthy cloth.

We all fade like a leaf,
and our iniquities, like the wind, take us away.
7 There is no one who calls on your name,
or attempts to take hold of you;
for you have hidden your face from us,
and have delivered us into the hand of our iniquity.
8 Yet, O LORD, you are our Father;
we are the clay, and you are our potter;
we are all the work of your hand.
9 Do not be exceedingly angry, O LORD,
and do not remember iniquity forever.
Now consider, we are all your people.

In the above scripture, the most appropriate verse to use with a Children's Sermon would be verse 9c: "Now consider, we are all your people."

Much of this scripture passage is about sin and God's forsaking the people of God. This theme is not appropriate for children. They must first learn to know, experience, and trust the love of God. Working on sin and feeling alienated from God—through our own sin—will not come until people are older and more mature, and have a greater understanding of, and experience with, God.

Children could understand Isaiah 64:9c in the theme of God's people, that is, "I am part of God's people"; "Others are also part of God's people."

**Possible ways of developing the Isaiah scripture:** If I were to use this scripture (Isa. 64:9c), I would probably begin with a tangible object that I already have. It is a stole that depicts in many colors children from around the world. I would let the children touch the stole and tell me what they see. I would then begin to ask, as I point to the children they have named, "Is this child part of God's people?" I would continue this for several times and then ask, "What does this tell you about God and God's people?" Then I would tie this into the first Sunday in Advent, when we celebrate the gift God sent, the baby Jesus, to all of God's people. I like to remind the children that the purple they see in the decorated sanctuary is a reminder to us that the baby Jesus was the Son of God, and a King for all times and all people. Purple is the color for kings and queens, princes and princesses.

(Another source for this particular fabric depicting children from around the world is on the Internet site: http://www.greatfabrics.com. "Children of the World Tapestry Fabric." You can buy a swatch of it for $5.)

The children's handout would have the title "We Are All God's People!" I would use my Print Shop program to find three or four faces of children with different skin colors and/or clothing to represent the many different people of the world, and of course, the scripture reference and the date of this Children's Sermon

An alternate idea would be to cut out and paste several pictures of different children, glue them onto a handout template, and make your own copies for handouts, again using cardstock if possible. (Or if you have The Print Shop or another computer program, you can probably find the pictures to put on your cardstock handouts.)

· · · · · · ·

### 2. Psalm 80:1–7, 17–19

1   Give ear, O Shepherd of Israel,
      you who lead Joseph like a flock!
    You who are enthroned upon the cherubim, shine forth
2       before Ephraim and Benjamin and Manasseh.
    Stir up your might,
      and come to save us!
3   Restore us, O God;
      let your face shine, that we may be saved.
4   O LORD God of hosts,
      how long will you be angry with your people's prayers?
5   You have fed them with the bread of tears,
      and given them tears to drink in full measure.
6   You make us the scorn of our neighbors;
      our enemies laugh among themselves.
7   Restore us, O God of hosts;
      let your face shine, that we may be saved...

17   But let your hand be upon the one at your right hand,
      the one whom you made strong for yourself.
18   Then we will never turn back from you;
      give us life, and we will call on your name.
19   Restore us, O LORD God of hosts;
      let your face shine, that we may be saved.

(Please see the Isaiah scripture notes above. Psalm 80 has some of the same pitfalls for a Children's Sermon as does the Isaiah scripture, with fewer ways in which to pick out one or two verses. I would recommend not using this particular passage, if at all possible.)

· · · · · · ·

### 3. Mark 13:24–37

24 "But in those days, after that suffering, the sun will be darkened, and the moon will not give its light, 25 and the stars will be falling from heaven, and the powers in the heavens will be shaken. 26 Then they will see 'the Son of Man coming in clouds' with great power and glory. 27 Then he will send out the angels, and gather his elect from the four winds, from the ends of the earth to the ends of heaven.

28 From the fig tree learn its lesson: as soon as its branch becomes tender and puts forth its leaves, you know that summer is near. 29 So also, when you see these things taking place, you know that he is near, at the very gates. 30 Truly I tell you, this generation will not pass away until all these things have taken place. 31 Heaven and earth will pass away, but my words will not pass away.

32 But about that day or hour no one knows, neither the angels in heaven, nor the Son, but only the Father. 33 Beware, keep alert; for you do not know when the time will come. 34 It is like a man going on a journey, when he leaves home and puts his slaves in charge, each with his work, and commands the doorkeeper to be on the watch. 35 Therefore, keep awake—for you do not know when the master of the house will come, in the evening, or at midnight, or at cockcrow, or at dawn, 36 or else he may find you asleep when he comes suddenly. 37 And what I say to you I say to all: Keep awake."

One possible verse to use for the Children's Sermon is verse 28, "From the fig tree learn its lesson: as soon as its branch becomes tender and puts forth its leaves, you know that summer is near."

The themes for this particular verse would be *Creation* (God has made everything) and *Providence* (God plans for a good world, i.e., God has an orderly system for the world). And of course, part of God's plan for a "good world" was the gift of God's son, baby Jesus, whose coming we await each year during Advent.

You could also tie in the color of the season, purple, with the fact that God's son, Jesus, is from God and is royalty. Purple is the color of royalty.

**Possible ways of developing the Mark scripture:** One way to have a visual, plus perhaps smell and taste, would be to bring in a branch of something (if you live in a climate where something is growing, or possibly bring in a potted houseplant). Be ready to speak about God's world, how this particular plant is a part of that world—whether it's used for beauty in the home, or has some miniature fruit on it (e.g., a hot-house fruit tree). Talk with the children about the ways that God cares for plants: sending rain, providing sunshine, giving knowledge to people who care for the plants in our world.

The handout could have "God Plans for a Good World" printed at the top of the card, with the date and the scripture. You might give this handout to the children so that they can add their own ideas of what God has given to the world. A simple stick-figure drawing of the nativity could also be a part of this handout. The children could take these cards home and, as a family, add some more pictures to illustrate how God has planned for a good world.

••••••••

### 4. 1 Corinthians 1:3–9

3 Grace to you and peace from God our Father and the Lord Jesus Christ. 4 I give thanks to my God always for you because of the grace of God that has been given you in Christ Jesus, 5 for in every way you have been enriched in him, in speech and knowledge of every kind—6 just as the testimony of Christ has been strengthened among you—7 so that you are not lacking in any spiritual gift as you wait for the revealing of our Lord Jesus Christ. 8 He will also strengthen you to the end, so that you may be blameless on the day of our Lord Jesus Christ. 9 God is faithful; by him you were called into the fellowship of his Son, Jesus Christ our Lord.

This scripture has the most potential for a good and memorable Children's Sermon for a number of reasons. There are several words with which children can relate fairly easily: grace, peace, give thanks, spiritual gift, faithful, fellowship, Jesus Christ, God. Of the possible scriptures for this Sunday, this one seems to be the most positive for young children.

### C. Immersing in the Chosen Scripture

- Read again 1 Corinthians 1:3–9 silently, savoring the words which you know that most children can understand.
- Read the scripture aloud, slowly, two more times. Pause between each reading. Did any of the words "jump off the page" at you? If so, note those words. Write them down on your paper.

- As you reflect on this passage; write down any thoughts, questions, or ideas you might have, such as, 'What does grace mean to us today?"
- Which verses/verse do you think would be most appropriate for a Children's Sermon?
- Offer the scripture as a prayer to God, such as the following:

> *Thank you, God, that you have graced us in the gift of your son, Jesus Christ. This gift has touched our lives in countless ways. We are strengthened by the life he led, the love and compassion he showed those around him, and by his sacrifice for us. Because of the ways he taught us about you and your love, we are always confident that we can tell you anything and you will still love us. Thank you, thank you, God. Amen.*

- Spend a few minutes in silence, asking God to bless your work in preparation and to give you any thoughts that would be helpful to you during this time.

### D. Theme(s)

I chose verse 4 ("I give thanks to my God always for you because of the grace of God that has been given you in Christ Jesus"), and based the rest of this Children's Sermon on it.

The theme is *Faith-Response:* Thank you, God; I love you, God; Help me; I'll help you; I'm happy. This particular scripture and theme will work well as a demonstration where children will get to use the senses of seeing, hearing, touching, and speaking.

### E. Materials Needed

- a family/church member for whom you are thankful (someone who likes children and is willing to be a part of the Children's Sermon; you will want to go through the scenario with that person ahead of time);
- an 8.5 x 11 piece of paper with 1 Corinthians 1:4 printed on it: "I give thanks to my God always for you because of the grace of God that has been given you in Christ Jesus" (1 Cor. 1:4).
- Optional, if needed: a folding chair on which the person for whom you are thankful can sit.

### F. Outline

- Show the children the paper with 1 Corinthians 1:4. Have them help you read it aloud.

- Tell the children about your friend/family member, why you are thankful to God for this person, the ways that you have seen God's grace (God's love) at work in that person, how they demonstrate the love of Jesus Christ to others ("I thank God for my friend Betty Ann. She is always here to help me when I need some extra help. She loves to work with me at church. She's always happy to be doing something to help others.")
- Tell the children that you are going to ask your friend Betty Ann to come forward so that you and the children can say a prayer for her, thanking God for who she is.
- When Betty Ann comes forward, she can either sit in the chair, or stand in a circle as you join hands with her. (If she sits down, you and the children can stand around her holding hands while you and the children pray.)
- Thank Betty Ann for coming forward; suggest to the children that they, too, can thank God for the special friends or family God has given them.
- Pray (asking the children to pray after you) a simple prayer such as the one below in the Index Card section.

### G. Handout Suggestion

Summary phrase: "Thank you, God, for friends." Pictures of boys and girls, so that all children can relate to the art. Include the scripture passage or perhaps just verse 4 of 1 Corinthians.

### H. Index Card

- Invite children forward and greet them
- Read 1 Corinthians 1:4, with children (on sign/large print)
- Tell about Betty Ann
- Invite Betty Ann forward
- Join hands and pray
- Remind children they can thank God for friends, family, etc.
- Give children the handout and pray:

*Thank you, God*
*for Betty Ann.*
*She loves you*
*very much.*
*We are thankful*
*that she helps our church*

*in so many ways.*
*In Jesus' name we pray,*
*Amen.*


## YEAR B, ADVENT 2

### A. Scriptures

Isaiah 40:1–11; Psalm 85:1–2, 8–13; 2 Peter 3:8–15a; Mark 1:1–8a

### B. Process of Selection

Read each scripture and write down possible verses to use with children.

### 1. Isaiah 40:1–11

1   Comfort, O comfort my people, says your God.
2   Speak tenderly to Jerusalem,
     and cry to her
  that she has served her term,
     that her penalty is paid,
  that she has received from the LORD's hand
     double for all her sins.
3   A voice cries out:
  "In the wilderness prepare the way of the LORD,
     make straight in the desert a highway for our God.
4   Every valley shall be lifted up,
     and every mountain and hill be made low;
  the uneven ground shall become level,
     and the rough places a plain.
5   Then the glory of the LORD shall be revealed,
     and all people shall see it together,
     for the mouth of the LORD has spoken."
6   A voice says, "Cry out!"
  And I said, "What shall I cry?"
  All people are grass,
     their constancy is like the flower of the field.
7   The grass withers, the flower fades,
     when the breath of the LORD blows upon it;
     surely the people are grass.
8   The grass withers, the flower fades;
     but the word of our God will stand forever.

9   Get you up to a high mountain,
        O Zion, herald of good tidings;
    lift up your voice with strength,
        O Jerusalem, herald of good tidings,
        lift it up, do not fear;
    say to the cities of Judah,
        "Here is your God!"
10  See, the Lord GOD comes with might,
        and his arm rules for him;
    his reward is with him,
        and his recompense before him.
11  He will feed his flock like a shepherd;
        he will gather the lambs in his arms,
    and carry them in his bosom,
        and gently lead the mother sheep.

The Isaiah scripture has four verses/phrases that would work well with the Children's Sermon:

- v. 1 "Comfort, O comfort my people, says your God."
- v. 2 "Speak tenderly . . ."
- v. 3 " prepare the way of the Lord . . ."
- v. 11 "He will feed his flock like a shepherd; he will gather the lambs in his arms, and carry them in his bosom, and gently lead the mother sheep."

If I were to use this scripture, I would probably tie the phrases from verses 1 and 2 with v. 11, the entire verse.

Children could understand these sections of Isaiah 40:1–11 as the great love and caring that God has for them and all people.

**Possible ways of developing the Isaiah scripture:** Talk about shepherds, and how shepherds care for their sheep, the kinds of things they need to do. A shepherd speaks tenderly at times to calm and to comfort the sheep when they are afraid of something. Sometimes a shepherd has to go looking for a sheep and carry it back to the flock. The handout could show a shepherd, have part of verse 11 on it, and the date. This might be a time to give the children their own "sheep" made of construction paper, with cotton ball wool glued on for ears and body. (And this would also be a great time to recruit a few people to help make these sheep).

• • • • • • •

**2. Psalm 85:1–2, 8–13**

1  LORD, you were favorable to your land;
    you restored the fortunes of Jacob.
2  You forgave the iniquity of your people;
    you pardoned all their sin...

8  Let me hear what God the LORD will speak,
    for he will speak peace to his people,
    to his faithful, to those who turn to him in their hearts.
9  Surely his salvation is at hand for those who fear him,
    that his glory may dwell in our land.
10  Steadfast love and faithfulness will meet;
    righteousness and peace will kiss each other.
11  Faithfulness will spring up from the ground,
    and righteousness will look down from the sky.
12  The LORD will give what is good,
    and our land will yield its increase.
13  Righteousness will go before him,
    and will make a path for his steps.

In this passage, verses 8b and c, and verse 10 could be used successfully for the basis of the Children's Sermon.

- v. 8 "for [God] will speak peace to his people, to his faithful, to those who turn to him in their hearts,"
- v. 10 "Steadfast love and faithfulness will meet; righteousness and peace will kiss each other."

Children would be able to relate to the idea that God seeks peace, not only the absence of war, but also that inner peace we have when we do turn to God in our hearts. Part of this peace comes from our steadfast love for, and faithfulness to, God. As we try to live a "righteous'" ("right with God") life we do feel a sense of calm inside.

**Possible ways of developing the Psalm passage:** Ask the children what peace means to them. Show them a visual of people who seem to be peacefully enjoying each other, perhaps at a picnic or sitting in their home or lying in bed listening to someone read a story to them. You could explain that peace does not always mean the absence of war. Sometimes we can find a peace within ourselves when we stay close to God in our hearts and minds. A handout in the shape

48    *The Children's Sermon*

of a heart, with verse 8 written on it, plus the reference and the date, would be a way to remember this particular Children's Sermon.

• • • • • • •

### 3. 2 Peter 3:8–15a

8 But do not ignore this one fact, beloved, that with the Lord one day is like a thousand years, and a thousand years are like one day. 9 The Lord is not slow about his promise, as some think of slowness, but is patient with you, not wanting any to perish, but all to come to repentance. 10 But the day of the Lord will come like a thief, and then the heavens will pass away with a loud noise, and the elements will be dissolved with fire, and the earth and everything that is done on it will be disclosed.

11 Since all these things are to be dissolved in this way, what sort of persons ought you to be in leading lives of holiness and godliness, 12 waiting for and hastening the coming of the day of God, because of which the heavens will be set ablaze and dissolved, and the elements will melt with fire? 13 But, in accordance with his promise, we wait for new heavens and a new earth, where righteousness is at home.

14 Therefore, beloved, while you are waiting for these things, strive to be found by him at peace, without spot or blemish; 15 and regard the patience of our Lord as salvation.

Possible verses or phrases to use for the Children's Sermon would include only a portion of verse 14: "to be found by God at peace, without spot or blemish."

I would recommend that you not choose to use this scripture because it really concentrates on the end times, which is a scary and inappropriate topic for the Children's Sermon.

• • • • • • •

### 4. Mark 1:1–8

1 The beginning of the good news of Jesus Christ, the Son of God. 2 As it is written in the prophet Isaiah,
   See, I am sending my messenger ahead of you,
      who will prepare your way;
3 the voice of one crying out in the wilderness:
   'Prepare the way of the Lord,
      make his paths straight.'"

4 John the baptizer appeared in the wilderness, proclaiming a baptism of repentance for the forgiveness of sins. 5 And people from the whole Judean countryside and all the people of Jerusalem were going out to him, and were baptized by him in the river Jordan, confessing their sins. 6 Now John was clothed with camel's hair, with a leather belt around his waist, and he ate locusts and wild honey. 7 He proclaimed, "The one who is more powerful than I is coming after me; I am not worthy to stoop down and untie the thong of his sandals. 8 I have baptized you with water; but he will baptize you with the Holy Spirit."

The Mark scripture has the most potential for providing an interesting and memorable scripture for this second Sunday in Advent for Year B, because (a) there are characters in this passage whom the children will already know or will get to know over the years; (b) this passage contains both good action and dialogue; (c) both the Isaiah passage and the Psalm make reference to some aspect of the story of John the "baptizer," (in case the person in charge of choosing the scripture does choose either Isaiah 40 or Psalm 85); and (d) this is a perfect passage in which to include another person from the congregation to help with the Children's Sermon.

### C. Immersing in the Chosen Scripture

- Read Mark 1:1–8 silently, savoring the words which you know that most children can understand.
- Read the scripture aloud, slowly, at least two times. Pause between each reading. Did any of the words "jump out" at you? Note those words. Write them down on your paper.
- Reflect on this passage, then write down any thoughts, questions, or ideas you might have.
- Which verses/verse do you think would be most appropriate for a Children's Sermon? Or do you think that this entire passage could be used as a story to be enacted by another person, or told by you? (Verses 4–8 actually tell the story of John the Baptist.)
- Offer the scripture as a prayer to God:

  *Thank you, God, for the story of your special messenger, John the Baptist, who was faithful to his calling as a messenger. We thank you that he paved the way for your Son, Jesus. We thank you for John's willingness to alert the Jewish people to the long-promised messiah now in their midst. In the name of Jesus we pray, Amen.*

- Spend a few minutes in silence, asking God to bless your work in preparation and to give you any thoughts that would be helpful to you during this time.

## D. Theme(s)

- *Hope; God's Self-Revelation*; God kept the promise made to the Jewish people of a Savior; God is good; God loves God's people. Centuries before the coming of John the Baptist, God had promised to send the Jewish people both a messiah (the anointed one of God) and a messenger to proclaim the way for the messiah. God kept the promise by sending John.
- *God loves all people.* God showed immense love for the Jewish people (God's people) by following through on the promise made long before this story in the gospel of Mark.

## E. Materials Needed

- someone to walk through the sanctuary dressed as John the Baptist might dress—in "camel's hair tunic" with a leather belt, proclaiming "Prepare the way of the Lord . . . make His paths straight!"
- a piece of fabric "fur" that might feel like camel's hair
- a leather belt
- a small container of honey with enough tasting sticks for each child
- a paper napkin for each child
- a paper bag to collect the used tasting sticks
- moist towels/towelettes, for the children to wipe sticky hands, mouths

## F. Outline

- Invite the children forward and welcome them.
- Immediately, "John the Baptist" walks through the sanctuary
- Ask the children, "Who do you think that was?" If the scripture was read before the Children's Sermon (and they were listening!), they might be able to answer, "John the Baptist." Older children might remember this person from hearing about him in previous times. However, if no one knows who he is, explain that this is John the Baptist, and why he was sent by God.

- As you tell a brief story about John, pass around the piece of fabric that might be similar to camel's hair and the belt for the children to feel. Give each child a paper napkin as you explain John's diet—locusts (kind of like crickets or grasshoppers) and honey. Dip the little tasting sticks into your container of honey and let each child taste. Collect the used paper napkins and tasting sticks. Give each child, as needed, a moist towelette, and then collect them.
- Ask the children to bow their heads and pray after you, using the prayer listed below on the index card.

### G. Handout suggestion

Summary phrase: "God sent John the Baptist to prepare people for Jesus, God's Son." Show a crooked path and a straight one, or something that looks like wilderness or a painting of John the Baptist.

### H. Index Card

- Invite children forward and greet them
- (John the Baptist walks by)
- Questions: Who was that? What do you know about him?
- Story points:
- Related to Jesus
- Lived in the desert
- Clothing/ fabric, leather
- Food/ honey
- Sent by God/ why . . .
- Give children handouts and pray, thanking God for John the Baptist:

*Thank you, God,*
*for John the Baptist.*
*He helped the people*
*get ready*
*for your Son, Jesus.*
*Help us to get ready*
*to celebrate Jesus' birth.*
*In Jesus' name we pray*
*Amen.*

## YEAR B, 2ND SUNDAY AFTER EPIPHANY

### A. Scriptures

1 Samuel 3:1–10, (11–20); Psalm 139:1–6, 13–18; 1 Corinthians 6:12–20; John 1:43–51

### B. Process of Selection

Read each scripture and write down possible themes and/or verses.

### 1. 1 Samuel 3:1–10 (11–20)

1 Now the boy Samuel was ministering to the LORD under Eli. The word of the LORD was rare in those days; visions were not widespread. 2 At that time Eli, whose eyesight had begun to grow dim so that he could not see, was lying down in his room; 3 the lamp of God had not yet gone out, and Samuel was lying down in the temple of the LORD, where the ark of God was. 4 Then the LORD called, "Samuel! Samuel!" and he said, "Here I am!" 5and ran to Eli, and said, "Here I am, for you called me." But he said, "I did not call; lie down again." So he went and lay down. 6 The LORD called again, "Samuel!" Samuel got up and went to Eli, and said, "Here I am, for you called me." But he said, "I did not call, my son; lie down again." 7 Now Samuel did not yet know the LORD, and the word of the LORD had not yet been revealed to him. 8 The LORD called Samuel again, a third time. And he got up and went to Eli, and said, "Here I am, for you called me." Then Eli perceived that the LORD was calling the boy. 9 Therefore Eli said to Samuel, "Go, lie down; and if he calls you, you shall say, 'Speak, LORD, for your servant is listening.'" So Samuel went and lay down in his place.

10 Now the LORD came and stood there, calling as before, "Samuel! Samuel!" And Samuel said, "Speak, for your servant is listening."

#### Themes

*God's Self-Revelation:* God called to Samuel, trying to get his attention.

*People of God:* Both Eli and Samuel were part of the people of God.

*Faith-Response:* Once Samuel realized it was God calling him, he answered, "Speak, for your servant is listening."

**Possible ways of developing the scripture:** Ask one or two people from the congregation to help you with this Children's Sermon. Have them call to one of the children, or to you. See if the children can recognize the voice without seeing the person(s) calling. Then tell a shortened story of Samuel and Eli.

• • • • • • •

### 2. Psalm 139:1–6, 13–18

1   O LORD, you have searched me and known me.
2   You know when I sit down and when I rise up;
       you discern my thoughts from far away.
3   You search out my path and my lying down,
       and are acquainted with all my ways.
4   Even before a word is on my tongue,
       O LORD, you know it completely.
5   You hem me in, behind and before,
       and lay your hand upon me.
6   Such knowledge is too wonderful for me;
       it is so high that I cannot attain it...

13   For it was you who formed my inward parts;
        you knit me together in my mother's womb.
14   I praise you, for I am fearfully and wonderfully made.
        Wonderful are your works;
     that I know very well.
15   My frame was not hidden from you,
     when I was being made in secret,
        intricately woven in the depths of the earth.
16   Your eyes beheld my unformed substance.
     In your book were written
        all the days that were formed for me,
     when none of them as yet existed.
17   How weighty to me are your thoughts, O God!
        How vast is the sum of them!
18   I try to count them—they are more than the sand;
        I come to the end—I am still with you.

**Themes:**

*Creation:* This psalm refers to God's amazing creation of humankind.

*Providence:* God watched over the psalmist even before the psalmist's birth.

*Hope:* The psalmist places his or her hope in God, for the present and the future.

**Possible ways of developing the passage:** Have the children demonstrate some things they can do with their bodies, as you direct them, such as, tiptoe, stretch, clap their hands, etc. Then talk about the marvelous ways in which God has created each of us.

• • • • • • •

### 3. 1 Corinthians 6:12–20

12 "All things are lawful for me," but not all things are beneficial. All things are lawful for me, but I will not be dominated by anything. 13 Food is meant for the stomach and the stomach for food, and God will destroy both one and the other. The body is meant not for fornication but for the Lord, and the Lord for the body. 14 And God raised the Lord and will also raise us by his power. 15 Do you not know that your bodies are members of Christ? Should I therefore take the members of Christ and make them members of a prostitute? Never! 16 Do you not know that whoever is united to a prostitute becomes one body with her? For it is said, "The two shall be one flesh." 17 But anyone united to the Lord becomes one spirit with him. 18 Shun fornication! Every sin that a person commits is outside the body; but the fornicator sins against the body itself. 19 Or do you not know that your body is a temple of the Holy Spirit within you, which you have from God, and that you are not your own? 20 For you were bought with a price; therefore glorify God in your body.

The only verses that could be suitable for the Children's Sermon are verses 19–20: "Or do you not know that your body is a temple of the Holy Spirit within you, which you have from God, and that you are not your own? For you were bought with a price; therefore glorify God in your body."

**Themes:**

*Creation:* God has created our bodies; as temples of the Holy Spirit, they belong to God.

People of God: Each person, every child belongs to the People of God.

*Hope:* Our hope is that God loves each of us very much!

*Faith-Response:* We respond to God's great love by trying to live as People of God.

**Possible ways of developing this passage:** I would not recommend this passage for use with the Children's Sermon. However, if it is chosen, use one of the above themes.

• • • • • • •

### 4. John 1:43–51

43 The next day Jesus decided to go to Galilee. He found Philip and said to him, "Follow me." 44 Now Philip was from Bethsaida, the city of Andrew and Peter. 45Philip found Nathanael and said to him, "We have found him about whom Moses in the law and also the prophets wrote, Jesus son of Joseph from Nazareth."

46 Nathanael said to him, "Can anything good come out of Nazareth?" Philip said to him, "Come and see." 47 When Jesus saw Nathanael coming toward him, he said of him, "Here is truly an Israelite in whom there is no deceit!" 48 Nathanael asked him, "Where did you get to know me?"

Jesus answered, "I saw you under the fig tree before Philip called you." 49 Nathanael replied, "Rabbi, you are the Son of God! You are the King of Israel!"

50 Jesus answered, "Do you believe because I told you that I saw you under the fig tree? You will see greater things than these." 51 And he said to him, "Very truly, I tell you, you will see heaven opened and the angels of God ascending and descending upon the Son of Man."

**Themes:**

*God's Self-Revelation:* Jesus revealed himself to Nathanael, who then believed in him.

*Faith-Response:* Nathanael became a follower of Jesus, one of his twelve disciples.

*Hope:* Both Philip and Nathanael began to hope that Jesus was the fulfillment of God's promises to God's people.

**Possible ways of developing this passage:** This would be an excellent time to talk with the children about the faith response which you celebrate in your church: (1) believers' baptism and confession of faith or (2) infant dedication or baptism. You could do this in several different ways. I have chosen to use one of those ways in the sections that follow.

### C. Immersing in the Chosen Scripture

- Read John 1:43–51 again, silently, lingering over the words which you know that most of the children will understand.
- Read the scripture aloud, slowly, at least two times. Ask yourself what words or phrases leaped out at you. Write those on your piece of paper or index card. Make notes of *why they caught your attention.*
- Reflect on this passage; then write down any thoughts, questions, or ideas you might have. What is most important to you about this passage? Why? What does it say for you as a follower of Jesus Christ today?
- Which verses/verse do you think would be most appropriate for a Children's Sermon?
- Offer the scripture as a prayer to God:

  *Thank you, God, for the unique ways in which Jesus called his disciples. Thank you for Philip, who became an early evangelist, bringing Nathanael with him to meet Jesus.*

  *Help me to be your evangelist also, a gentle evangelist, as I work with the children who come forward for the Children's Sermon. Guide me into the thoughts I need and the direction this particular Children's Sermon needs to go. Thank you for your help always! In Jesus' name, Amen.*

- Spend a few minutes in silence, asking God to bless your work in preparation and to give you any thoughts that would be helpful to you during this time.

### D. Themes

- *God's Self-Revelation:* God, through Jesus, revealed himself to the two men, Philip and Nathanael; he was able to see Nathanael even before he met him.
- *Faith-Response:* Earlier Nathanael was so completely 'turned off' by the idea of someone important coming out of Nazareth that he would barely listen to Philip. But once Jesus told Nathanael things about him that Jesus should not have been able to know, Nathanael's attitude completely changed, and

he exclaimed, "Rabbi, you are the Son of God! You are the King of Israel!"

- *Hope:* Both Philip and Nathanael experienced much hope in Jesus as the promised Messiah, the Son of God.

### E. Materials Needed

- Picture of a baptism
- Bowl of water
- Hand towel

### F. Outline

- Invite the children to come forward as you greet them with hospitality.
- Tell a simple version of Jesus calling his disciples.
- Ask, "Do you know how people join our church? What they do? What they say?" (Give the children a minute or two to answer your questions; if you don't get any responses, share some of the following information. Adapt where it does not fit with the practices in your own congregation.) Our minister invites those who wish to do so to come to the front of the sanctuary and join this church. We sing a song of invitation. The minister introduces the people who have come forward, one by one. The minister holds the person's hand and asks him or her, "Do you believe that Jesus is the Christ, the Son of the living God, and do you take him for your Savior and Lord?" The person will say, "I do," or "yes." The minister welcomes the person into the church, as a member. And if the person has never been baptized, then at a later time that person is baptized. (Note: If you will be having a baptism in the near future, invite your children to be present for it.)
- While you are saying the above words, let the children dip their hands into the water and then dry them with the hand towel. (This could be a place in which to use a helper to hold the pan, and the towel while you are telling the story about your church and how people join your church.)
- Ask the children to pray with you the prayer below.

### G. Handout Suggestions

Summary phrase: "Jesus called his disciples and Jesus still calls us today." Use pictures of Jesus and his disciples and of a baptism.

## H. Index Card

- Invite children forward; greet them
- Our scripture: Jesus asked Philip to follow him; Philip invited a friend, Nathanael, to follow.
- Questions: Does Jesus call disciples today to follow him? How do people show that they want to follow Jesus? How do people join our church?
- Story Points:
- Nathanael and Philip were friends.
- Philip wanted to introduce Nathanael to Jesus.
- Nathanael decided to follow Jesus and become a disciple.
- Tell how people become part of our church (Pass the water around, and the towel)
- Give children handouts and pray:

*Thank you, God, for Jesus*
*and his disciples.*
*Thank you for our church*
*and our minister.*
*Thank you when people*
*decide to join our church.*
*We love you, God.*
*In Jesus' name we pray.*
*Amen.*

## YEAR B, LENT 1

### A. Scriptures

Genesis 9:8–17; Psalm 25:1–10; 1 Peter 3:18–22; Mark 1:9–15

### B. Process of Selection

Read each of the four scriptures slowly, and ask God to help you choose which one of these would work well as the basis for a Children's Sermon.

After you have had some experience of working through the longer process of selection (carefully reading and praying about each scripture, looking for possible themes and ways to present this scripture as a Children's Sermon), you are probably ready to do the quicker form of choosing a scripture. For this, you will also read each scripture slowly, but you'll be able to discern through prayer which one or two scriptures might lend themselves very well for the basis of the Children's Sermon.

After reading the above four scriptures for the first Sunday in Lent, I chose the Mark scripture because it is about Jesus–his baptism, his days of temptation in the wilderness, and his going out to proclaim the Good News. Each of the other three scriptures could be developed, but I felt that this one lent itself best for a Children's Sermon on the first Sunday in Lent.

Read your chosen scripture again, slowly.

> [9]In those days Jesus came from Nazareth of Galilee and was baptized by John in the Jordan. [10]And just as he was coming up out of the water, he saw the heavens torn apart and the Spirit descending like a dove on him. [11]And a voice came from heaven, "You are my Son, the Beloved; with you I am well pleased." [12]And the Spirit immediately drove him out into the wilderness. [13]He was in the wilderness forty days, tempted by Satan; and he was with the wild beasts; and the angels waited on him. [14]Now after John was arrested, Jesus came to Galilee, proclaiming the good news of God, [15]and saying, "The time is fulfilled, and the kingdom of God has come near; repent, and believe in the good news." (Mk. 1:9–15)

What are the themes for children in this passage?

*God's Self-Revelation:* God certainly employed a self-revelation by sending Jesus into the world and especially at Jesus' baptism when the Spirit-dove descended upon him and the voice from heaven proclaimed, "You are my Son, the Beloved; with you I am well pleased." In children's terms: Jesus is good; Jesus let himself be tempted, but did not sin.

*Sin:* Jesus spent days in the wilderness being tempted by Satan to sin, which he did not do. In children's terms: God is pleased when we do not sin.

*People of God:* Both John and Jesus are people of God. In children's terms: Children belong to the People of God.

*Providence:* God sent Jesus into the world to make the world a better place.

*Hope:* Jesus gives us much hope.

What verses are especially meaningful for children? The Mark passage contains many good verses that would have meaning for the children. I have chosen vs.14b (Jesus came to Galilee, proclaiming the good news of God) on which to base the Children's Sermon.

What are the most effective learning methods that could be used with this passage? In this Children's Sermon, the children will listen, see, touch, and experience as they learn some more about what it means to "proclaim the Good News of God."

### C. Immersing in the Chosen Scripture

- Read the Mark passage again, silently, lingering on the words which you know that most of the children will be able to understand.
- Read the scripture aloud, slowly, at least two times. As you read the scripture, read it first from *the viewpoint of John the Baptist.* You have been preaching to the people in the Judean countryside, following your call from God to get them ready, get them prepared for someone who will follow you. Then your cousin Jesus shows up. Place yourself in John's body as you read this scripture. Next, read it from *the viewpoint of the people at the Jordan River that day,* people who were just watching the goings-on and those who had come to earnestly hear this strange preacher from the wilderness. What would you feel when this scripture began to happen? Finally, read it *as one living today,* in the twenty-first century. How does this scripture touch you where you are today?
- Reflect on this passage, then write down any thoughts, questions, or ideas that you might have. *Do not neglect this step.* It is important, for where you have questions, some of the children may also have questions. For example, if John the Baptist really was one of God's People, why was he arrested? (This does not mean that you're going to go on all of the little "side trips" as you try to answer lots of questions. Rather, it just makes you aware of some things that might be going through the children's minds.)
- Which verses/verse do you think would be most appropriate for a Children's Sermon? I have already shared with you that I shall be using v.14b for this particular Children's Sermon. You may decide to use another one. *Always* feel free to *do this,* because *you know your group of children better than do I,* their needs, their interests, their capabilities, etc.
- Offer the scripture as a prayer to God:

    *Thank you, God, for your love and your providence. I know how much you want the children in our congregation to get to know you better. Help me during this planning time to craft this Children's Sermon so that it will be the best possible way to bring our children into a meaningful time with you. Help them learn to love, to trust, and to depend on you in their lives. All these things I ask in the name of your precious son, Jesus, Amen.*

- Spend a few minutes in silence, asking God to bless your work in preparation, and to give you any thoughts that would be helpful to you during this time.

## D. Themes

Chosen Theme: I shall use the theme of *Hope* (God always keeps God's promises, as related to the Good News of Jesus Christ). I would approach this through learning and sharing a little about what Good News actually is.

## E. Materials Needed

- Picture of Jesus helping someone (see list of possible sources in Appendix B).
- Bible
- Handout cards to share with congregation
- Handout cards for children to keep

## F. Outline

- Invite the children forward
- Greet them as they sit down around you
- Review, briefly, the story in Mark: When Jesus was an adult, he went to the Jordan River and asked his relative, John the Baptist, to baptize him
- As Jesus came out of the water, a dove descended, and a voice called Jesus his beloved Son.
- Jesus went to the wilderness and stayed forty days; he continued to pray and stay close to God
- Then he was ready to tell everyone the Good News of God's love
- Ask: What do you suppose Jesus said or did to convince people that God loved them?
- Today you're going to get a chance to share the Good News in our church.
- Explain: Each of you will have two cards (show and read) and you are to give one of these to someone after we have our prayer.

- What is the Good News we have to share? (That God loves you!)
- Pray with children the prayer below.

### G. Handout Suggestion

Summary phrase: "Jesus came to Galilee to tell the Good News of God." Use picture of Jesus healing someone with a simple Good News statement such as, "God loves you." Give each child two handouts, one to keep and one to give to someone in the congregation.

### H. Index card.

- Invite children forward; greet them
- Tell story of Jesus' baptism briefly.
- Say: after being baptized and spending time in the wilderness, Jesus was ready to tell everyone the Good News of God's love
- Ask: What do you suppose Jesus said or did to convince people that God loved them?
- What is the Good News we have to share? (That God loves you!)
- Say: Today you're going to get a chance to share the Good News in our church.
- Explain: Each of you will have two cards (show and read) and you are to give one of these to someone after we have our prayer.
- Give children handouts and pray:

  *Thank you, dear God,*
  *for sending Jesus to us!*
  *Thank you for the ways*
  *he told others of your love!*
  *Thank you for helping us*
  *as we tell others*
  *of your love for them.*
  *In Jesus' name we pray. Amen.*

### YEAR B, LENT 3

### A. Scriptures

Exodus 20:1–17; Psalm 19; 1 Corinthians 1:18–25; John 2:13–22

## B. Process of Selection

Read each of the four scriptures slowly, and ask God to help you choose which one of these would work well as the basis for a Children's Sermon.

By now you'll be able to discern through prayer which one or two scriptures might lend themselves very well for the basis of the Children's Sermon.

This is one of the weeks when all four scriptures have very positive teachings that could be used for the Children's Sermon. Here are some possibilities:

**Exodus 20**—You could concentrate on one particular commandment as you tell this story; you could set a scene in which you act out breaking one of the commandments with another member of the congregation (e.g., you take something that belongs to that person; then you apologize to the person and talk through the event with the children).

**Psalm 19**—A beautiful psalm of praise and thanksgiving for both God's creation and the gift of laws that help us live, this passage also has many possibilities. A picture of a beautiful scene from nature could provide a good visual. (This is where collecting calendar pictures comes in handy.) Talking with the children about the importance of a particular law with which they are familiar, such as crossing streets only at crosswalks and with the traffic, could help them to appreciate how important laws can be to our safety and peace of mind.

**John 2**—This is the story of Jesus cleansing the temple because of how those in charge had begun to desecrate this holy place of God through their overcharging and cheating persons who desired to have a closer relationship with God. This could be demonstrated by two or more church members who come walking through the sanctuary, talking loudly and completely ignoring your time with the children. You could talk with the children about their feelings when this was happening (and it would be a good idea to have those same people come back to "apologize," telling them that they were asked to do this as part of the Children's Sermon!)

**1 Corinthians 1**—This scripture might be the most difficult to use because of its concept of a powerful king versus a loving, suffering savior. Yet this can also be used effectively in a Children's Sermon, which I will demonstrate in this session.

· · · · · · ·

Read your chosen scripture again, slowly.

18 For the message about the cross is foolishness to those who are perishing, but to us who are being saved it is the power of God. 19 For it is written,

"I will destroy the wisdom of the wise,
    and the discernment of the discerning I will thwart."

20 Where is the one who is wise? Where is the scribe? Where is the debater of this age? Has not God made foolish the wisdom of the world? 21 For since, in the wisdom of God, the world did not know God through wisdom, God decided, through the foolishness of our proclamation, to save those who believe. 22 For Jews demand signs and Greeks desire wisdom, 23 but we proclaim Christ crucified, a stumbling block to Jews and foolishness to Gentiles, 24 but to those who are the called, both Jews and Greeks, Christ the power of God and the wisdom of God. 25 For God's foolishness is wiser than human wisdom, and God's weakness is stronger than human strength." (1 Cor. 1:18–25)

What are the themes for children in this passage?

- *God's Self-Revelation*: Through the apostle Paul, God revealed the reason for using the cross to bring good news to all of God's people. Paul's inspired writings begin to make sense to Christians as to why God ignored the "wisdom" of the world, knowing that human wisdom never compares with the heavenly, spiritual, all-knowing wisdom of God. In children's language, "God is good; God does what is best and good for me/us."
- *Judgment*: God has always given people free choice: for the Greeks to choose wisdom and for the Jews to demand signs. In children's language, "We can choose to believe that what God did through Jesus Christ was good for us and for all people everywhere."
- *People of God*: Paul belongs to the People of God; each of us belongs to the People of God; we are God's children.
- *Providence*: God's plans, through Jesus, are for a better world.

What verses are especially meaningful for children?

- verse. 20a: Where is the one who is wise?

- verse 21a: For since, in the wisdom of God, the world did not know God through wisdom, God decided, through the foolishness of our proclamation, to save those who believe.
- verse 25: For God's foolishness is wiser than human wisdom, and God's weakness is stronger than human strength.

What are the most effective learning methods that could be used with this passage?

- Listening, seeing (visual/picture of destruction through power, such as a Super Villain)
- touching (small wooden cross or a nail)

### C. Immersing in the Chosen Scripture

- Read the scripture aloud, slowly, at least two times, looking for the words that will have special meaning for the children in your group. Read one sentence at a time and pause. Try to picture in your mind and in your heart what Paul is saying. Picture, if you can, God thinking and deciding what is the best way to touch people's lives through his son, Jesus.
- Reflect on this passage, then write down any thoughts, questions, or ideas you might have.
- Which verses/verse do you think would be most appropriate for a Children's Sermon?
- Offer the scripture as a prayer to God:

  *Wise and thoughtful God, you always know our minds and our feelings. Help me to better understand your plan for salvation through the cross. Help me to know a simple way in which I can explain just a little about this to the children. Give me wisdom and insight. Give me yearning to know the best way to approach this Children's Sermon. And I continue to bring you my love and adoration. In Jesus' name, Amen.*

- Spend a few minutes in silence, asking God to bless your work in preparation, and to give you any thoughts that would be helpful to you during this time.

### D. Chosen Theme(s)

*Providence:* God did, through wisdom and love, what was and is good for the world. Instead of using brute force to make people believe (and afraid to not believe!), God used the love of Jesus, who gave his life willingly so that we might know how very much God loves us.

### E. Materials Needed

- Bible
- Picture of evil villain (comic book character) or destruction (destroyed buildings)
- A wooden cross (the rougher hewn, the better, small enough to pass around and touch), and/or a couple of large nails
- Handout for each child

### F. Outline

- Call the children forward, and greet them with hospitality
- Ask the children how many weeks until Easter (four)
- Tell them that a lot of people still have trouble understanding Easter
- Show picture of comic book villain or destruction of a building
- Explain that some people only understand power that can lead to bad things: hurting other people; forcing people to do what you want them to do
- Show the wooden cross (or the nails), and then pass them around the group as you tell talk about the scripture
- From your Bible, read   1 Corinthians 1:25: "For God's foolishness is wiser than human wisdom, and God's weakness is stronger than human strength."
- Say, "God is wiser than the wisest person who ever lived; God knew that force was not the answer. Our wise God chose love to be stronger than either power or force. That's why God sent Jesus into the world as a helpless baby. That's why Jesus gave his life for us. Because he and God love us. They love everyone in the world so much that Jesus was willing to die on a cross to show his love. We may not understand this. We don't have to. Jesus showed us God's love for you and me and for all people. This love of Jesus has changed the world."
- Read the handout, and then give one to each child.
- Pray with children.

### G. Handout Suggestion

Summary phrase: "Thank you, God, for being so wise." Include picture of something strong and put an X through it. Show picture of simple cross.

### H. Index Card

- Call children forward, and greet them

- Ask: How many weeks until Easter? (four)
- Explain strength/power of cross versus strength/power as we usually think of it.
- Show the wooden cross (or the nails), and then pass them around
- Read from Bible 1 Corinthians 1:25:
- Say, "God is wiser than the wisest person who ever lived,"
- Emphasize how the cross shows God's wisdom and love.
- Read the handout, and then give one to each child.
- Pray:

*Thank you, God, for the gift of your son Jesus.*
*Thank you for the love*
*he showed for each person.*
*And, thank you, God,*
*for being so wise!*
*In Jesus' name, Amen.*

## YEAR B, PALM SUNDAY

### A. Scriptures

Psalm 118:1–2, 19–29; Mark 11:1–11; John 12:12–16

### B. Another Process of Selection

By now you are probably ready to do the quicker form of choosing a scripture. Read each of the four lectionary scriptures slowly. You'll be able to discern through prayer and past experience which one or two scriptures might lend themselves very well for the basis of the Children's Sermon. Because your children are best known to you (and not to this writer), you will be able to determine what they might relate to best, what they need to hear (based on what is happening in their individual lives and the collective life of your congregation), and the learning styles that they have.

Any of the three scriptures listed above would be possible beginnings for this week's Children's Sermon. Below are the three scriptures and how I might use them if I were doing this Sunday's Children's Sermon. (Note: I only included three; many more are listed for this day.)

**Psalm 118:1–2, 19–29:** I would probably choose verse 24: "This is the day that the LORD has made; let us rejoice and be glad in it." This is a verse that has been made into a praise song, thus providing an opportune way to involve the whole congregation. After reading this verse aloud to the children (from the *New Revised Standard Version Bible*), you could have your organist/pianist invite the choir and congregation to sing this song through a couple of times. I would spend a few minutes asking the children what is important about this particular Sunday. (If you have a palm parade, they will be ready to share!)

*Note:* It would also be good planning to have the children already familiar with this song. Perhaps others who work with them, either in Sunday school, Children's Worship, or Children's Extended Session, might be able to sing this song with them in the weeks before Palm Sunday. You would also want to alert your church musicians of your need for their help and support in singing this. If you or someone you know can play a guitar, this would also be a good accompaniment to this praise song.

**Mark 11:1–11** and **John 12:12–16** tell the story of Jesus on Palm Sunday. The Mark passage goes into preparation details, while the John passage is shorter and sticks mainly to the parade, with an author's comments from hindsight. I chose John for its brevity and will concentrate on verses 13 and 14.

Read your chosen scripture again, slowly, and aloud.

12 The next day the great crowd that had come to the festival heard that Jesus was coming to Jerusalem. 13 So they took branches of palm trees and went out to meet him, shouting,

"Hosanna!
    Blessed is the one who comes in the name of the Lord—
        the King of Israel!"

14 Jesus found a young donkey and sat on it; as it is written:

15 "Do not be afraid, daughter of Zion.
Look, your king is coming, sitting on a donkey's colt!"

16 His disciples did not understand these things at first; but when Jesus was glorified, then they remembered that these things had been written of him and had been done to him. (Jn. 12:12–16)

What are the themes for children in this passage?

*Redemption:* The Greek word *Hosanna,* means "Please save" or "Save now." It indicates that on the first Palm Sunday the Jewish people were looking for one to save them, whether from their sins or, more likely, from living under the Roman oppressors. This could be a good tie-in for the children as they learn the meaning of the word *Hosanna*. Please save me; save me now.

*Providence:* This is one more story in which God planned for a good world, and wanted/wants to help care for all people in the world. Children can understand "God loves me; God cares for me."

*Hope:* God had promised a savior to the Jewish people. God always keeps promises that God has made. God has given a savior to me also. God will always be with me, no matter what happens. God loves me very much.

What verses are especially meaningful for children?

Verse 13 would be especially meaningful to the children because they have most likely heard it before:

> So they took branches of palm trees and went out to meet
> him, shouting, "Hosanna!
> Blessed is the one who comes in the name of the Lord—
> the King of Israel!"

What are the most effective learning methods that could be used with this passage?

- Listening
- Touching and holding a palm leaf
- Retelling the story of Palm Sunday
- Singing a song and waving palm branches

### C. Immersing in the Chosen Scripture

- Read John 12:12–16 silently, thinking about the various learning methods that are possible with children of this age: listening, seeing, touching, smelling, tasting, experiencing, or a combination of all of these. Perhaps you have some ideas about other learning methods. Be assured that you know your children better than this writer, and you can feel confident to try another learning method if you believe it would help them draw closer to God through this particular scripture passage.
- Read the scripture aloud, slowly, at least two times. As you read this scripture passage aloud the first time, put yourself into those long-ago times. You are a person who has heard of Jesus indirectly and you want to see him. So you grab your palm leaf and join the crowd. What do you see? What do you hear? How do you feel? In the second oral reading, come

back to today. You are a child in your congregation. What does this scripture mean to you? Have you ever walked (or been carried) in a palm parade? If so, how did you feel? How do you feel? What do you understand about this parade? What questions do you have, as a child?

- Reflect on this passage, then write down any thoughts, questions, or ideas you might have.
- Which verses/verse do you think would be most appropriate for a Children's Sermon?
- Offer the scripture as a prayer to God:

*Thank you, God, that you inspired the writers of our gospels so long ago. Thank you for their words, which have come down through the centuries. What a blessing! Help me to feel what happened that day so long ago when the people in Jerusalem welcomed Jesus with so much enthusiasm, and then, so soon afterward, turned against him. Lest I be judgmental, help me to remember times when I, too, have turned against Jesus, or at least looked the other way when he was asking me to help. Give me better vision, stronger will, and more powerful love for you and your son. Fill me with your Holy Spirit. Amen.*

- Spend a few minutes in silence, asking God to bless your work in preparation and to give you any thoughts that would be helpful to you during this time.

### D. Chosen Theme(s)

*Hope, Providence,* and *People of God* are the major themes for this day, not only for the children, but for all the youth and adults who are present in the worship service on Palm Sunday. I chose to focus on the theme of Hope.

### E. Materials Needed

- Bible
- Piece of paper (8.5 x 11, lengthwise) with the word HOPE written on it
- Words to "This Is the Day" (or check your hymnal for this song)
- Pianist/organist, choir to help congregation sing "This Is the Day"
- Palm leaves, one for each child to hold
- Handout for each child

## F. Outline:

- Invite the children to come forward; greet them with hospitality
- Ask them if they know what this day is (Palm Sunday)
- Why do we celebrate this day?
- Hold up the word HOPE
- Explain that HOPE describes Palm Sunday very well. The people in the crowd that day had hope that Jesus had come to save them. And he had! But many of them wanted an earthly king to save them from their enemies. Jesus had come to save them in another way, to let them know how much God loved them, and to help them learn how to love God in better ways. God sent Jesus to show us God's love and to help us know what is good. Jesus wants to help us know what is right and what is wrong and help us do the right. Jesus is the HOPE in the world!
- We're going to sing a song, a joyful song that reminds us about this day long ago.
- The words are: This is the day / that the Lord has made / we will rejoice / and be glad in it. (If song is familiar or is in your hymnals, invite everyone to sing it. If not, have a small group sing it once, let people join in when they can, and sing it two times. Note: "This Is the Day" is in the *Chalice Hymnal*, no. 286).
- Give each child a palm leaf and a handout. (After the prayer, they can walk back to their seats, or leave for Extended Worship, Children's Worship, nursery care, etc., waving their palm leaves, while everyone sings "This Is the Day" one more time.)

## G. Handout Suggestion

Summary phrase: "This is the day which the Lord has made." Show picture of Palm Sunday scene with Jesus on a donkey and people waving palm branches.

## H. Index Card

- Invite children to come forward; greet them
- What is today?
- Hold up the word HOPE, explain connection to Palm Sunday
- Sing hopeful, joyful song: "This Is the Day."

- Give each child a palm leaf and a handout.
- Pray:

*Thank you, God,*
*for this day you have made!*
*Thank you for Jesus*
*who came to give us hope!*
*We love you, God.*
*In Jesus' name we pray, Amen.*

(After the prayer, they can walk back to their seats, or leave for Extended Worship, Children's Worship, nursery care, etc., waving their palm leaves, while everyone sings "This Is the Day" one more time.)

# CHAPTER 8

# Sample Children's Sermons, Lectionary Year C

## YEAR C, LENT 5

### A. Scriptures

Isaiah 43:16–21; Psalm 126; Psalm 119:9–16; Philippians. 3:4b–14; John 12:1–8

### B. Process of Selection

Read each scripture; write down themes and possible verses to use in the Children's Sermon.

### 1. Isaiah 43:16–23

16  Thus says the LORD,
    who makes a way in the sea,
    a path in the mighty waters,
17  who brings out chariot and horse,
    army and warrior;
    they lie down, they cannot rise,
    they are extinguished, quenched like a wick:
18  Do not remember the former things,
    or consider the things of old.
19  I am about to do a new thing;
    now it springs forth, do you not perceive it?
    I will make a way in the wilderness
    and rivers in the desert.
20  The wild animals will honor me,
    the jackals and the ostriches;
    for I give water in the wilderness,

        rivers in the desert,
     to give drink to my chosen people,
21    the people whom I formed for myself
       so that they might declare my praise.
22   Yet you did not call upon me, O Jacob;
       but you have been weary of me, O Israel!
23   You have not brought me your sheep for burnt offerings,
       or honored me with your sacrifices.
    I have not burdened you with offerings,
       or wearied you with frankincense.

In these verses, three verses or phrases would work well with the Children's Sermon: verses 19–21, all of which are positive descriptions of how God will care for God's people and all of God's creation. The children would especially relate to verse 20, where the wild animals will honor God because God is providing water for them to drink in the wilderness.

One way to use this scripture, with the themes of Creation and Providence, would involve bringing three or four carved, wooden figures of wild animals, particularly if you could find or borrow a jackal and an ostrich as two of the carved animals.

After reading verse 20, show the figures you have of wild animals, and then pass them around for the children to examine and touch while you continue telling the rest of the Children's Sermon.

One point to make is that if God is so caring about the wild animals God has created, how much more does God want to also care and provide for each of us? For each of them?

•••••••

## 2. Psalm 126

1   When the LORD restored the fortunes of Zion,
     we were like those who dream.
2   Then our mouth was filled with laughter,
     and our tongue with shouts of joy;
    then it was said among the nations,
      "The LORD has done great things for them."
3   The LORD has done great things for us,
     and we rejoiced.
4   Restore our fortunes, O LORD,
     like the watercourses in the Negeb.
5   May those who sow in tears
     reap with shouts of joy.

6   Those who go out weeping,
        bearing the seed for sowing,
    shall come home with shouts of joy,
        carrying their sheaves.

In Psalm 126, verse 5 ("may those who sow in tears reap with shouts of joy") might be used to talk about hard times as opposed to good times. This verse definitely lifts up themes of Hope, Providence, and Faith-Response.

Glue a paper plate onto a stick (a tongue depressor). Use markers to draw a happy face on one side and a sad face on the other side. Using these two faces, talk with the children about times when we feel sad and times when we feel happy. An additional handout for this Children's Sermon (in addition to the usual postcard with a graphic, part of the scripture, the scripture reference, and date) could be a paper plate glued on a stick, along with a couple of crayons so they can draw their own happy/sad faces.

Two points to emphasize are: (1) God loves us at all times, and (2) God is always with us.

• • • • • • •

### 3. Psalm 119:9–16

9   How can young people keep their way pure?
        By guarding it according to your word.
10  With my whole heart I seek you;
        do not let me stray from your commandments.
11  I treasure your word in my heart,
        so that I may not sin against you.
12  Blessed are you, O LORD;
        teach me your statutes.
13  With my lips I declare
        all the ordinances of your mouth.
14  I delight in the way of your decrees
        as much as in all riches.
15  I will meditate on your precepts,
        and fix my eyes on your ways.
16  I will delight in your statutes;
        I will not forget your word.

This portion of Psalm 119 is concerned with both knowing and keeping God's laws. Important verses to emphasize would be verses 10–12, especially: "with my whole heart I seek you; do not let me stray from your commandments; I treasure your word . . .; teach me your statutes (laws)." If we do not know God's laws, or commandments (or God's will) for our lives, we cannot possibly keep them.

One way of presenting this, if it is at all possible, would be to borrow a mezuzah or a phylactery from a synagogue or Jewish friend. The mezuzah is what Jews place on the doors leading into their homes as a reminder that they should always remember the Jewish prayer, "Shema Yisrael" ("Hear, O Israel, the Lord is our God, the Lord alone (or is One)" [Deut. 6:4]. You could make a representative of this by taking a piece of heavyweight paper, approximately 3 x 5", and write on the inside, "I am the Lord your God; you shall have no other gods before me." Roll it tightly into a cylinder. If you have a container about that size, place the rolled-up scroll in the container. This would be a great project for creative folks in the church to help make a facsimile for each child to take home.

Include in this Children's Sermon talking with the children about what they can do in their homes to remember who God is and what God wants us to be and to do. A postcard handout is also important to remind them of what they learned this day.

· · · · · · ·

### 4. Philippians 3:4b–14

If anyone else has reason to be confident in the flesh, I have more: 5 circumcised on the eighth day, a member of the people of Israel, of the tribe of Benjamin, a Hebrew born of Hebrews; as to the law, a Pharisee; 6 as to zeal, a persecutor of the church; as to righteousness under the law, blameless. 7 Yet whatever gains I had, these I have come to regard as loss because of Christ. 8 More than that, I regard everything as loss because of the surpassing value of knowing Christ Jesus my Lord. For his sake I have suffered the loss of all things, and I regard them as rubbish, in order that I may gain Christ 9 and be found in him, not having a righteousness of my own that comes from the law, but one that comes through faith in Christ, the righteousness from God based on faith. 10 I want to know Christ and the power of his resurrection and the sharing of his sufferings by becoming like him in his death, 11 if somehow I may attain the resurrection from the dead. 12 Not that I have already obtained this or have already reached the goal; but I press on to make it my own, because Christ Jesus has made me his own. 13 Beloved, I do not consider that I have made it my own; but this one thing I do: forgetting what lies behind and straining forward to what lies ahead, 14 I press on toward the goal for the prize of the heavenly call of God in Christ Jesus.

This scripture is the least usable for the Children's Sermon. Trying to explain or demonstrate even a phrase of it would take more time than what you have available for the children. If this scripture is chosen by someone else, your best tactic would probably be to use the verses from Psalm 126.

• • • • • • • •

### 5. John 12:1–8

1 Six days before the Passover Jesus came to Bethany, the home of Lazarus, whom he had raised from the dead. 2 There they gave a dinner for him. Martha served, and Lazarus was one of those at the table with him. 3 Mary took a pound of costly perfume made of pure nard, anointed Jesus' feet, and wiped them with her hair. The house was filled with the fragrance of the perfume. 4 But Judas Iscariot, one of his disciples (the one who was about to betray him), said, 5 "Why was this perfume not sold for three hundred denarii and the money given to the poor?" 6 (He said this not because he cared about the poor, but because he was a thief; he kept the common purse and used to steal what was put into it.) 7 Jesus said, "Leave her alone. She bought it so that she might keep it for the day of my burial. 8 You always have the poor with you, but you do not always have me."

This scripture has the most potential for providing an interesting and memorable scripture because it is an action scripture, filled with characters.

One good way to present this would be to tell the story and have some things to see, touch, taste, and smell along the way, such as dates or raisins, food at the table, perfume (costly perfume) for anointing, and coins or money to give or to hoard.

### C. Immersing in the Chosen Scripture

- *Read silently.* Read the John scripture again, slowly and silently, keeping aware of things that are confusing or amazing to you.

Keep in mind the various ways in which children learn best, particularly those that involve their senses of touch, smell, taste, sight, sound, or a combination of several of these.

- *Read the scripture aloud, slowly, at least two times.* The *first time,* picture the entire biblical scene in this story at a sweep: Where are Martha and Mary? Where are Jesus and the other disciples? Where is Lazarus? (Remember that the men reclined as they gathered around a table, in biblical times; the women served, but normally did not eat at the table with the men.) The *second time,* pay close attention to the *conversation* and who says what.
- *Reflect on this passage,* then write down any thoughts, questions, or ideas you might have.
- *Which verse or verses* do you think would be most appropriate for a Children's Sermon?
- Offer the scripture as a prayer to God:

  *Loving God, as I read this scripture, I realize that times are not so different today from the days of Jesus and his disciples. We still let greed keep us from giving generously. We still find fault with others who love you. Be with me as I read and meditate upon this scripture. Thank you, God. In Jesus' name I offer this prayer, Amen.*

- *Spend a few minutes in silence,* asking God to bless your work in preparation, and to give you any thoughts that would be helpful to you during this time.

### D. Theme(s)

- *God's Self-Revelation through Jesus:* Jesus revealed three important things in this passage: (1) Mary was preparing Jesus for his burial (whether she actually knew it or not) ; (2) Jesus was not afraid to stand up for women; and (3) the world will always have its poor people because many of us have not learned to share who we are and what we have. Children will understand that God is good; God loves all people; Jesus loves everyone.
- *Sin:* Even asking the question about the "poor," Judas caused Jesus to feel sorrow. Jesus, of course, knew Judas's heart. Children can understand that sin does disappoint God.
- *Judgment:* It mattered very much what Judas said and what Judas did. It matters what we say and do also.
- *Redemption:* However, God loves everyone, even sinners.

Especially sinners! Children need to know that God loves them, even when they do something that is not right.

### E. Materials Needed

- Bible
- Tangibles to illustrate parts of the story: dates or raisins (or loaf of freshly baked bread); a bottle of inexpensive perfume; a cloth bag with some coins inside (enough to jangle)
- One handout for each child

### F. Outline

- Invite the children to come forward; greet them with hospitality.
- Introduce the Bible story by showing them, in the Bible, John, chapter 12.
- Points to make: Jesus and his disciples were eating with Mary, Martha, Lazarus (*pass food*). Mary began to anoint Jesus' feet, using some expensive perfume (*perfume*). Judas, one disciple, began to complain: "That money should be given to the poor!! Why waste it on someone's feet?" (*money bag with coins*). Jesus knew that Judas was stealing, spending some of their money. But Jesus said, "Mary is doing a good thing. She is using her costly perfume to prepare me for burial." (*Briefly explain custom.*)
- How do you think Jesus felt when Mary anointed his feet? When Judas complained?
- Give children their handouts and pray with them.

### G. Handout Suggestion

Summary phrase: "Mary, sister of Martha, shared her love for Jesus."

### I. Index Card/Outline

- Invite children forward and greet them.
- Tell story of Mary, Jesus, and Judas.
  Jesus and disciples were eating with Mary, Martha, Lazarus (*food*). Mary begins to wash Jesus' feet with perfume (*perfume*). Judas gets upset. Jesus knows Judas steals money at times (*bag with coins*). Jesus praises Mary; anointing him for burial (*explain custom*). How did Jesus feel when Mary washed his feet? When Judas complained?

- Give children handouts and pray::

*We thank you, God, for Mary,*
*the sister of Martha*
*and Lazarus.*
*Thank you for her love*
*she shared with Jesus.*
*Teach us how to*
*be more loving.*
*In Jesus' name we pray.*
*Amen.*

## YEAR C, EASTER 2

### A. Scriptures

Acts 5:27–32; Psalm 150; Revelation 1:4–8; John 20:19–31

### B. Process of Selection

Read each scripture and write down possible verses to use with children.

### 1. Acts 5:27–32

27 When they had brought them, they had them stand before the council. The high priest questioned them, 28 saying, "We gave you strict orders not to teach in this name, yet here you have filled Jerusalem with your teaching and you are determined to bring this man's blood on us." 29 But Peter and the apostles answered, "We must obey God rather than any human authority. 30 The God of our ancestors raised up Jesus, whom you had killed by hanging him on a tree. 31 God exalted him at his right hand as Leader and Savior that he might give repentance to Israel and forgiveness of sins. 32 And we are witnesses to these things, and so is the Holy Spirit whom God has given to those who obey him."

The above scripture occurs in the middle of a story. This is the story of Peter and other followers of Jesus who had been warned by the Jerusalem high authorities to quit preaching and teaching in the name of Jesus. Probably the most appropriate verse to use with a Children's Sermon would be verse 20: "But Peter and the apostles answered, 'We must obey God rather than any human authority.'"

Children could understand that sometimes our Christian beliefs will go against what others around us want to do themselves, or even want us to do.

**Themes:**

*Judgment:* What we do really does matter; what Peter and the other apostles did, when they continued to tell others about Jesus the risen Savior, really did matter. Because of them, we are Christians today.

*People of God:* We belong to the People of God; Peter and the other disciples also belonged to the People of God.

*Faith-Response:* We give God thanks for the people we read about in the Bible, especially those who continued to tell about Jesus. Because of Peter and others like him, we know the Good News of God's love through Jesus Christ.

**Possible ways of developing this scripture:** This scripture lends itself to thinking and talking about how we tell others about Jesus Christ as God's Good News. It would be a good time to have a demonstration on this, not only for the children but also for the congregation. One way to do this is to role play a scene with one of your older, more outgoing children. You will need to talk with this child beforehand so he or she has time to think about how he or she would invite a good friend to come to church as a guest. Involve the parents to help with this.

The day's handout might be titled, "Invite a Friend to Church Next Week!" Underneath you could list some possible ways to approach this, plus a picture of a church and/or church people. If you have access to a photograph of your church (perhaps from the church Web site), you could have your church on the handout, also.

• • • • • • •

### 2. Psalm 118:14–29 or Psalm 150

(Psalm 118 was used for Year B, Palm Sunday. Refer to chapter 7 even if you choose to use Psalm 118 for the Children's Sermon).

### 3. Psalm 150

1    Praise the LORD!
     Praise God in his sanctuary;
         praise him in his mighty firmament!
2    Praise him for his mighty deeds;
         praise him according to his surpassing greatness!

3   Praise him with trumpet sound;
        praise him with lute and harp!
4   Praise him with tambourine and dance;
        praise him with strings and pipe!
5   Praise him with clanging cymbals;
        praise him with loud clashing cymbals!
6   Let everything that breathes praise the LORD!
    Praise the LORD!

In the above scripture, the psalmist is going "all out" to praise God. This would be a great opportunity to have the children use rhythm instruments to sing a song, march around the sanctuary, and play their rhythm instruments. If you choose a well-known song, such as "Do, Lord," or "When the Saints Go Marching In," the congregation might sing along with the children, or at least clap their hands in time to the music.

Children can understand that through our songs, our movements, and musical instruments, we do praise God, and with enthusiasm!

Themes:

*Faith-Response,* especially "I'm happy!" But also, "Thank you, God."

*People of God,* including the fact that even the children can lead something special during the worship service because they are, indeed, part of the People of God!

Since I have chosen this one for the Children's Sermon, I will go into a few more details further in this session.

· · · · · · ·

### 3. Revelation 1:4-8

4 John to the seven churches that are in Asia: Grace to you and peace from him who is and who was and who is to come, and from the seven spirits who are before his throne, 5 and from Jesus Christ, the faithful witness, the firstborn of the dead, and the ruler of the kings of the earth. To him who loves us and freed us from our sins by his blood, 6 and made us to be a kingdom, priests serving his God and Father, to him be glory and dominion forever and ever. Amen.

7 Look! He is coming with the clouds;
    every eye will see him,
even those who pierced him;
    and on his account all the tribes of the earth will wail.

So it is to be. Amen.

8 "I am the Alpha and the Omega," says the Lord God, who is and who was and who is to come, the Almighty.

•••••••

The one possible verse to use for the Children's Sermon is verse 8, "I am the Alpha and the Omega," says the Lord God, who is and who was and who is to come, the Almighty."

Using signs on which you have printed the Greek letters for Alpha (α, A) and Omega (ω, Ω), plus the English words *Alpha* and *Omega,* you could begin teaching them these four Greek symbols. Since our New Testament was originally written in Greek, it would be good for children to begin recognizing some of the symbols for the various letters of the Greek alphabet. Alpha and Omega are especially important because we use and hear them frequently in our faith discussions.

**Themes:**

*Creation:* God has always been; God will always be; God created everything.

*Providence:* God's plans for a good world mean that God will always be present.

*Hope:* God will always be with me, for God is "forever and ever, without end."

•••••••

### 4. John 20:19–31

19 When it was evening on that day, the first day of the week, and the doors of the house where the disciples had met were locked for fear of the Jews, Jesus came and stood among them and said, "Peace be with you." 20 After he said this, he showed them his hands and his side. Then the disciples rejoiced when they saw the Lord. 21 Jesus said to them again, "Peace be with you. As the Father has sent me, so I send you." 22 When he had said this, he breathed on them and said to them, "Receive the Holy Spirit. 23 If you forgive the sins of any, they are forgiven them; if you retain the sins of any, they are retained." 24 But Thomas (who was called the Twin), one of the twelve, was not with them when Jesus came. 25 So the other disciples told him, "We have seen the Lord." But he said to them, "Unless I see the mark of

the nails in his hands, and put my finger in the mark of the nails and my hand in his side, I will not believe." 26 A week later his disciples were again in the house, and Thomas was with them. Although the doors were shut, Jesus came and stood among them and said, "Peace be with you." 27 Then he said to Thomas, "Put your finger here and see my hands. Reach out your hand and put it in my side. Do not doubt but believe." 28 Thomas answered him, "My Lord and my God!" 29 Jesus said to him, "Have you believed because you have seen me? Blessed are those who have not seen and yet have come to believe." 30 Now Jesus did many other signs in the presence of his disciples, which are not written in this book. 31 But these are written so that you may come to believe that Jesus is the Messiah, the Son of God, and that through believing you may have life in his name.

• • • • • • •

This scripture has potential for a great Children's Sermon, for it tells the story of our lives in this age: "Do not believe it unless you can see it!" Or, "Do not believe all that you hear or see!" This could be enacted by two church members portraying Jesus and Thomas. A simple dialogue could be composed for this; then you could discuss with the children what they saw and heard (or what they thought they saw and heard).

**Themes:**

*God's Self-Revelation:* God made one of the biggest revelations of self ever during these two appearances of Jesus to the disciples in the upper room.

*God's Redemption:* God, through Jesus, continued to love Thomas, even though Thomas had some issues with belief.

*Providence:* God demonstrated the master plan for the world through the resurrection of Jesus.

*Hope:* This sacred scripture brings hope to all the world, but the children's hope would be how faithful God is in keeping promises, and that God has made a glorious plan in which God will always take care of us.

### C. Immersing in the Chosen Scripture

- Read again silently Psalm 150, picturing in your mind the sights and the sounds contained in this musical psalm.

- *Read the scripture aloud, slowly, two more times. The first time,* listen carefully to any words you think the children may not know very well, such as *firmament.* What does *firmament* mean to you? Picture the various instruments as you read their names: trumpet, lute, harp, tambourine, strings, pipe, cymbals. Are you familiar with these named instruments? (And strings, of course, could be guitars or violins or mandolins, etc.) The *second time,* picture your group of children circling through the sanctuary while they sing and play their rhythm instruments. Can you picture the congregation as they join in and also help to "praise the Lord"?
- As you reflect on this passage write down any thoughts, questions, or ideas you might have, and then ponder the answers to each of them.
- *Which verse or verses do you think would be most appropriate* for a Children's Sermon? Mark those verses so that you will remember them.
- Offer the scripture as a prayer to God:

  *What a joy it is, O God, when we get together to worship you in our sanctuary! Be with me as I plan for some kind of joyful celebration with the children leading our praises to you. Touch the hearts of our church people that they might enter into this special time with our children. Please continue to guide me in your wisdom through this process. In Jesus' name I pray, Amen.*

- *Spend a few minutes in silence, asking God to bless your work in preparation* and to give you any thoughts that would be helpful to you during this time.

### D. Theme(s)

- *Faith-Response,* especially "I'm happy!" But also, "Thank you, God."
- *People of God,* including the fact that even the children can lead something special during the worship service because they are, indeed, part of the People of God!

Both of these themes will play a significant part in this Children's Sermon.

### E. Materials Needed

- Bible
- rhythm instruments, one for each child if possible (you can

be creative and include some homemade instruments, such as two pan lids; a pan lid and a large metal or wooden spoon). If you have access to an educational toy store, you can usually get a number of instruments at fairly low cost, and they are normally well-constructed and should last a long time.
- a handout for each child

### F. Outline

- Invite the children forward; greet them with hospitality.
- Read Psalm 150 aloud, then repeat verse 1b: "Praise God in his sanctuary!"
- Ask, "What does this mean? How do we praise God in our sanctuary?"
- Tell them that today they will be leading a praise time. Give each child a rhythm instrument (and you will need one also!). Explain the song you will be singing with the congregation (make sure it is one most people will know, such as "This Little Light of Mine," "When the Saints Go Marching In," or "Do, Lord"). In a music situation, it always a good idea to make sure that you give the organist/pianist and/or the choir director a week or two advance notice that you are going to be doing something requiring music. By doing this, you will have one good group of people supporting you!
- Lead the children around the sanctuary as you sing and play rhythm instruments, then come back to your place in the front. (Also, depending on the number of children you have, it's good to recruit a parent or teacher helper for this activity to help in handing out instruments, gathering instruments afterward, and following the procession to "herd" any stragglers).
- Give  children the handout; go over it with them, then have them pray with you.

### G. Handout Suggestion

Summary phrase: "Praise God in the Sanctuary!" Use pics of musical instruments.

### H. Index Card

- Invite the children forward; greet them
- Read Psalm 150 aloud
- Repeat "Praise God in his sanctuary!"

- Ask: "What does this mean? How do we praise God in our sanctuary?"
- Distribute musical instruments
- Lead the children around the sanctuary as you sing familiar song
- Give children the handout and pray:

  *Thank you, God,*
  *for this church,*
  *for the people here today,*
  *for a time to praise you*
  *with our voices and our instruments!*
  *We love you, dear God!*
  *In Jesus' name, Amen.*

## YEAR C, EASTER 4

### A. Scriptures

Acts 9:36–43; Psalm 23; Revelation 7:9–17; John 10:22–30

### B. Process of Selection

Read each of the four scriptures slowly, and ask God to help you choose which one of these would work well as the basis for a Children's Sermon.

By now you are ready to read each scripture slowly and discern through prayer and past experience which one or two scriptures might lend themselves very well for the basis of the Children's Sermon.

- The Acts scripture tells the story of Peter raising a Christian woman, Dorcas, from the dead. This scripture could be problematic for young children, especially those who have experienced a death in the family. If this scripture is chosen for you, one way to work with this would be to emphasize that Dorcas was remembered by all her friends and church family with much love because of the way she shared her love with others.
- Psalm 23 is the well-known Shepherd's Psalm, "The Lord is my shepherd." There are many good verses to emphasize: vs. 1–3, God's providence; v. 4, God is with me at all times; and v. 6, I will always be with God, and God will be with me.

- Revelation 7:9–17 tells about the multitude from all the nations. Revelation is definitely *not* a child's book. Many adults have misunderstood and misused this biblical book through the ages. If the person who chooses the scriptures begins to preach a series on Revelation, my best advice is for you to do some general stories from the Bible, using, perhaps, one of the Children's Bibles as a starting point. *(See Appendix B for suggested children's books.)*
- John 10:22–30 is the story of Jesus being rejected by some of the Jewish people. Both the John scripture and Psalm 23 have some of the same themes, and would be the easiest for children to understand. I have chosen the John scripture, but much of what is listed below could also be adapted quite easily to Psalm 23.

Read your chosen scripture again, slowly.

At that time the festival of the Dedication took place in Jerusalem. It was winter, and Jesus was walking in the temple, in the portico of Solomon. So the Jews gathered around him and said to him, "How long will you keep us in suspense? If you are the Messiah, tell us plainly." Jesus answered, "I have told you, and you do not believe. The works that I do in my Father's name testify to me; but you do not believe, because you do not belong to my sheep. My sheep hear my voice. I know them, and they follow me. I give them eternal life, and they will never perish. No one will snatch them out of my hand. What my Father has given me is greater than all else, and no one can snatch it out of the Father's hand. The Father and I are one." (Jn. 10:22–30)

What are the themes for children in this passage?

*God's Self-Revelation:* Through Jesus, God was saying to this particular group, "If you really want to know who this man is, then follow him. Listen to him. See what he does." For children, this translates as, "I know that God is good. Jesus is good. We need to listen to his words and watch all that he does."

*Judgment:* What we do really does matter to God. The decisions we make to either follow the teachings of Jesus or to not follow Jesus' teachings will affect the rest of our lives. Listening to the words of scripture helps us to see and to know Jesus more clearly.

What verses are especially meaningful for children?

Verse 27: "My sheep hear my voice. I know them, and they follow me." Children can relate to this, especially if they have a dog at home. They also know that very young children recognize the voices of their mothers and fathers, sisters and brothers, and others with whom they spend time.

What are the most effective learning methods that could be used with this passage?

- Listening
- Experiencing (acting out, playing a game)

## C. Immersing in the Chosen Scripture

- Read John 10:22–30 again, silently and slowly. Think about how the children will be best able to understand this scripture. In addition to the various themes and ideas of presenting those themes, which senses will best be implemented for most effective learning by the children?
- Read the scripture aloud, slowly, two more times. The *first time*, concentrate on the Jews who wanted to know, very badly, whether or not Jesus was the Messiah. Listen to Jesus' reply. Why do you think he said what he did? The *second time* you read this scripture aloud, put yourself into Jesus' mind and listen carefully to what those people were asking you. How do you feel about them? Why do you say what you do in response?
- Reflect on this passage; then write down any thoughts, questions, or ideas you might have.
- Which verses/verse do you think would be most appropriate for a Children's Sermon?
- Offer the scripture as a prayer to God:

  *I know, most loving God, that you sent Jesus to be the Good Shepherd to me. You desire that I listen to his voice, and that I learn from him. How blessed I am to be able to read his words and actions and teachings in my Bible! Help me to find the right words so that the children with whom I work will also hear the voice of Jesus. Thank you, God, for your love, which continues to undergird all that I try to do. In Jesus' name, Amen.*

- Spend a few minutes in silence, asking God to bless your work in preparation, and to give you any thoughts that would be helpful to you during this time.

## D. Theme(s)

*God's Self-Revelation.* Children can understand this theme as God wanting to be a part of their lives. God wants them to recognize when God is calling them; children can learn to recognize God in their lives if they begin to know who God is through learning about Jesus.

## E. Materials Needed

- Bible
- one handout for each child
- three adults to say a phrase, "Come and Follow Me," out of sight of the children (but well-amplified so that their voices are loud enough to be heard throughout the sanctuary)

## F. Outline:

- Invite the children to come forward; greet them with hospitality
- If children have just heard the scripture read, you will need to only repeat v. 27, "My sheep hear my voice. I know them, and they follow me."
- Ask if anyone has a dog. If so, what do they do to get the dog to come to them? (Call them by name? They know their name and you, so they come to you.)
- Explain that in the Bible story for today, Jesus was being questioned by people who did not follow him. In fact, they probably had no desire to follow him. Jesus told them that his followers knew him; they knew his voice; they knew what he was trying to teach them; they believed him; and they followed him.
- Explain that you're going to play a game called "Come and Follow Me." Rules: everyone closes their eyes and listens to the voice, which will say, "Come and follow me." You will say the names of three church members who may have been the voice (using three fairly-known women's names in the congregation if the speaker is a woman, or three men's names for a male speaker). As soon as the children recognize the speaker they just heard, they are to raise their hands. Explain that they will do this three times. When the speakers have been guessed, tell the children that sometimes it's difficult to know who is speaking, even when we are listening. Jesus especially wants us to listen to him and learn to follow him in our Sunday school time, in Worship, when we read the

Bible at home, during the Children's Sermon, even during the Adult Sermon.
- Thank the children for playing the game.
- Give children the handout; go over it with them.
- Invite the children to bow their heads and pray after you.

### G.. Handout Suggestion

Summary phrase: "My sheep hear my voice." Use picture of Jesus and children.

### I. Index Card

- Invite children forward; greet them
- Dogs; how do you call them?
- Play a game, "Come and Follow Me"
- Explain rules; do three voices (give them 3 possible choices)
- Give children handouts and pray:

  *Thank you, God, for Jesus!*
  *Help us learn*
  *to follow him.*
  *Help us listen*
  *to his voice.*
  *In Jesus' name we pray,*
  *Amen.*

## YEAR C, EASTER 6

### A. Scriptures

Acts 16:9–15; Psalm 67; Revelation 21:10, 21:22–22:5; John 14:23–29; John 5:1–9

### B. Process of Selection

Read each of the five scriptures slowly, and ask God to help you choose which one of these would work well as the basis for a Children's Sermon.

By now you can read each scripture slowly and then discern through prayer and past experience which one or two scriptures might lend themselves very well for the basis of the Children's Sermon.

The Acts scripture (Acts 16:9–15) tells the delightful story of Paul receiving his call (his vision) to go to Macedonia to proclaim the Good News to people in that area. It also includes the story of Lydia, the seller of purple cloth. Stories (narratives) are usually good beginnings for the Children's Sermon. One interesting way to present this is to have a costumed storyteller. Another is to have a tangible item, such as a piece of purple fabric. This scripture lifts up themes of Redemption, People of God, Providence, Hope, and Faith-Response.

Psalm 67 may be very familiar to you. The first two verses are often used for benedictions. Almost any of the verses would work very well for the basis of the Children's Sermon. As you consider your children's needs and the church situation, choose one or two on which to concentrate. This should provide plenty of ideas for both the theme and the possible ways to make that verse or verses come alive for the children.

The Revelation scripture, as explained in the previous session (Easter 2), is not really suitable for young children.

John 14:23–29 has elements that are very good for setting the stage for upcoming Pentecost Sunday, especially verse 26, "but the Advocate, the Holy Spirit, whom the Father will send in my name." This scripture also has a couple of excellent ideas about the concept of peace: "Peace I leave with you; my peace I give to you. I do not give to you as the world gives. Do not let your hearts be troubled, and do not let them be afraid" (v. 27).

This could provide an excellent Children's Sermon about both feelings (fear) and how one achieves some semblance of inner peace, even while the world around you is in turmoil. The children could understand this emphasis through the themes of Providence and Hope.

John 5:1–9 is the story of Jesus healing the man who had been ill for thirty-eight years. This man stayed close to a healing pool, but he could never be the first person to get into the "healing waters" after the waters had been stirred. According to tradition, the first person to step into the pool after the waters had been stirred would be healed. This story emphasizes themes of Providence, Hope, and Faith-Response.

• • • • • • •

Read your chosen scripture again, slowly. I have chosen the Acts scripture for this particular Sunday.

9 During the night Paul had a vision: there stood a man of Macedonia pleading with him and saying, "Come over to Macedonia and help us." 10 When he had seen the vision,

we immediately tried to cross over to Macedonia, being convinced that God had called us to proclaim the good news to them. 11 We set sail from Troas and took a straight course to Samothrace, the following day to Neapolis, 12 and from there to Philippi, which is a leading city of the district of Macedonia and a Roman colony. We remained in this city for some days. 13 On the sabbath day we went outside the gate by the river, where we supposed there was a place of prayer; and we sat down and spoke to the women who had gathered there. 14 A certain woman named Lydia, a worshiper of God, was listening to us; she was from the city of Thyatira and a dealer in purple cloth. The Lord opened her heart to listen eagerly to what was said by Paul. 15 When she and her household were baptized, she urged us, saying, "If you have judged me to be faithful to the Lord, come and stay at my home." And she prevailed upon us. (Acts 16:9–15)

What are the themes for children in this passage?

*Redemption:* When Lydia became a follower of Jesus, she immediately knew and experienced the redeeming qualities of the relationship with him. She was forgiven. She became a new person. Children relate to this theme by knowing that God loves them all the time, even when they do things they shouldn't–even when they don't do the things they should do.

*People of God:* Lydia and the other women who came down to the river to worship were a part of the People of God. Paul helped them to formalize that relationship by telling them about Jesus Christ. Children understand this as belonging to God's family and being a part of the church.

*Providence:* God's plan for a good world included putting Paul and Lydia together. Both of them were valuable in the spread of the Good News of Jesus Christ.

*Hope:* Our hope, as Christians, comes through depending and relying upon the promises of God. Lydia experienced this. The children also experience hope in God and in the promises of God.

*Faith-Response:* Lydia showed her thanks by opening her home to Paul and his traveling companions. This was her way of thanking God for what Paul had shared with her and her household. Children learn to pray and say, "Thank you, God," for the many blessings God has given to them. At this age, one of the best prayers we can teach the children is "Thank you, God."

What verses are especially meaningful for children?

- verse 14d: "The Lord opened her heart to listen eagerly to what was said by Paul;
- verse 15b: "If you have judged me to be faithful to the Lord, come and stay at my home."

What are the most effective learning methods that could be used with this passage?

- Listening to the story.
- Seeing the purple fabric.
- Touching the fabric.
- Taking home a piece of purple fabric on their handouts.

### C. Immersing in the Chosen Scripture

- Read silently, again, Acts 16:9–15.
- Read the scripture aloud, slowly, at least two times. *The first time* try to experience this scripture as Paul did during his vision as he slept. What would this have felt like to you? How would you know that this vision/urging came from God? (You may want to read a few verses before this passage to help with this answer). *The second time*, read the passage from Lydia's viewpoint. Have you been missing something in your life? How would Paul's Good News of God's love through Jesus Christ be an answer to your yearning? How would you feel after your baptism? Why would you invite Paul and his fellow travelers to stay with you in your home?
- Reflect on this passage. Then write down any thoughts, questions, or ideas you might have.
- Which verse or verses do you think would be most appropriate for a Children's Sermon? (Actually, the entire story can be used as the basis of the Children's Sermon.)
- Offer the scripture as a prayer to God:

  *Thank you, God, for this story of Lydia in the Bible. A wealthy woman, Lydia knew that she needed something more. She was looking for it, and then you brought Paul into her presence so he could share the Good News with her! May Lydia be an example of how I too have needs in my life. May this always be a reminder that I, like Lydia, am not beyond your love and your reach. In Jesus' name, Amen.*

- Spend a few minutes in silence, asking God to bless your work in preparation and to give you any thoughts that would be helpful to you during this time.

### D. Chosen Theme(s)

*Faith-Response.* Children can understand, in verse 15, how Lydia made a wonderful faith response after her baptism by Paul. She invited him and his group into her home to stay while they were in her city.

This is one of those opportunities to remind children that because God loves us, we can reach out to others in love.

### E. Materials Needed

* Bible
* one large (size of a hand towel, perhaps) piece of purple fabric
* possibly a person who will tell the story as Lydia
* a handout for each child, including a small piece of purple fabric

### F. Outline

* Invite the children to come forward; greet them with hospitality
* Show the children your large piece of purple fabric; pass it around for them to touch while you tell the following story (or have someone dress as Lydia and tell the story): A wealthy woman who lived a few years after Jesus died owned a business, making purple dye for clothing. Now only wealthy people could afford this purple clothing, which was costly because the dye for it came from a particular shellfish.
  Lydia worshiped God faithfully every Sabbath. One Sabbath she met a religious man named Paul. He told her about Jesus Christ. She believed in Jesus. Paul baptized her and her entire household, including family members and servants.
  Lydia was so thankful for Paul telling her about Jesus that she invited Paul and his friends to stay in her home!
* Show the handouts; give one to each child and pray.

### G. Handout suggestion

Summary phrase: "Lydia hears the Good News of Jesus." Use purple on card, perhaps picture of purple fabric. Show picture of woman being baptized.

## H. Index Card

- Invite children; greet them
- Show purple fabric
- Tell story of Lydia as fabric is passed
- Give children handouts and pray:

*Thank you, God, for Lydia,*
*and for this Bible story.*
*Help us to learn*
*ways to show others*
*our love for them.*
*Thank you, also,*
*for the apostle Paul,*
*who shared the Good News*
*with Lydia.*
*In Jesus' name, Amen.*

## YEAR C, PROPER 5

### A. Scriptures

1 Kings 17:8–16; Psalm 146; Galatians 1:11–24; Luke 7:11–17

### B. Process of Selection

Read each of the four scriptures slowly, and ask God to help you choose which one of these would work well as the basis for a Children's Sermon.

You should read each scripture slowly and then discern through prayer and past experience which one or two scriptures might lend themselves very well for the basis of the Children's Sermon.

The 1 Kings scripture (17:8–16) tells the compassionate story of Elijah's going to stay with a widow and her son in a time of great need. Elijah, speaking for God, tells the woman to not be afraid, but to follow his instructions and  share her food with him. This passage illustrates themes of Providence, Hope, and Faith-Response.

Psalm 146, a psalm of praise and entreaty to God for help, contains many themes, including Creation, Judgment, Redemption, People of God, Providence, and Hope.

The Galatians (1:11–24) passage tells of Paul's conversion (in his own words) from being a persecutor of Christians to being a confirmed believer and missionary for Jesus Christ. Themes include

God's Self-Revelation, Sin, Judgment, Redemption, People of God, and Faith-Response.

The passage from the gospel of Luke (7:11–17) is the story of Jesus and his disciples going to the town of Nain, encountering a widow whose only son had died, and Jesus' restoring the son to life. Themes include God's Self-Revelation, People of God, Providence, Hope, and Faith-Response.

All four of the passages could be developed into a Children's Sermon fairly easily, with the Luke passage being just a little more difficult because of Jesus raising the widow's son to life. I have chosen the Galatians passage, partly because it offers a good time to tell about the apostle Paul. But even more important, it is an opportunity to point out to the children that even some of the most famous and important people in the Bible sinned and had to turn their lives around so that they could serve God in better ways.

Read your chosen scripture again, slowly.

11 For I want you to know, brothers and sisters, that the gospel that was proclaimed by me is not of human origin; 12 for I did not receive it from a human source, nor was I taught it, but I received it through a revelation of Jesus Christ. 13 You have heard, no doubt, of my earlier life in Judaism. I was violently persecuting the church of God and was trying to destroy it. 14 I advanced in Judaism beyond many among my people of the same age, for I was far more zealous for the traditions of my ancestors. 15 But when God, who had set me apart before I was born and called me through his grace, was pleased 16 to reveal his Son to me, so that I might proclaim him among the Gentiles, I did not confer with any human being, 17 nor did I go up to Jerusalem to those who were already apostles before me, but I went away at once into Arabia, and afterwards I returned to Damascus. 18 Then after three years I did go up to Jerusalem to visit Cephas and stayed with him for fifteen days; 19 but I did not see any other apostle except James the Lord's brother. 20 In what I am writing to you, before God, I do not lie! 21 Then I went into the regions of Syria and Cilicia, 22 and I was still unknown by sight to the churches of Judea that are in Christ; 23 they only heard it said, 'The one who formerly was persecuting us is now proclaiming the faith he once tried to destroy.' 24 And they glorified God because of me. (Gal. 1:11–24)

What are the themes for children in this passage?

*God's Self-Revelation:* Paul claimed that the way in which he received the Gospel was through a direct encounter with the risen Lord while Paul was traveling to Damascus to persecute Christians. Children understand this theme as "God is good; God loves me; Jesus loves me."

*Sin:* Paul wrote in verse 13, "I was violently persecuting the church of God and was trying to destroy it." Paul spent his ministry confessing his prior sins against Christ's Church. Children understand sin as "doing wrong disappoints God; doing wrong hurts me; doing wrong hurts others."

*Judgment:* Paul knew that God had set him apart for something, and it was not to persecute Christians. Finally, through his encounter with Jesus Christ, he realized what God was calling him to do. For children, judgment is knowing that what we do really does matter. We live with the outcomes of our choices. God gives us the ability to make choices.

*Redemption:* Only through admitting that Jesus Christ had redeemed him through his crucifixion was Paul able to move ahead with his life. Children's understanding of redemption includes "God loves me all the time; God loves me even when I do wrong; God loves me when I'm good and when I'm not so good."

*People of God:* Paul talked about being a part of the People of God, even though he worked very independently at times. For children this theme plays out as belonging to God's family and being a part of the Church.

*Faith-Response:* Paul made a response in faith when he agreed to be a missionary for Jesus Christ. Children understand that thanking God is one way to respond in faith.

What verses are especially meaningful for children?

Verse 13 is a good verse with which to begin, telling the story of Paul's persecution of the Church. Verses 15–16 give a short history of how Paul came to know the risen Jesus Christ. Verses 23–24 testify to the fact that many believers had heard of Paul and his conversion and had praised God because of this.

What are the most effective learning methods that could be used with this passage?

- Listening and Seeing
- Touching
- Experiencing

## C. Immersing in the Chosen Scripture

- Read Galatians 1:11–24 again silently. Picture the children who usually come forward for the Children's Moment. What will they be able to understand best in this passage? How will you be able to work with the themes of sin, judgment, and redemption in a creative way, while still emphasizing God's love for them?

- Read the scripture aloud, slowly, at least two times. During the *first reading*, put yourself in Paul's circumstances when he is still persecuting the churches, but suddenly realizes that he is sinning against God. How do you feel? What do you want to do at that point in your life? During the *second reading*, picture yourself as having been forgiven for the things you have done against God's churches. What are your feelings now, about yourself, about what you have done, about your future as God's missionary? Then think of yourself as a child and something you did that made you feel guilty. What could someone have said to you to convince you that God loved you, even when you did something that God did not like?

- Reflect on this passage; then write down any thoughts, questions, or ideas you might have. As you concentrate on the questions or things you don't understand about this passage, write them down. This will help you be more effective as you work on the presentation of the Children's Sermon for any given week.

- Which verses/verse do you think would be most appropriate for a Children's Sermon? As stated earlier, verses 13, 15–16, and 23–24 would be good for telling the "before and after" stories of Paul. These would help provide children with the model of someone who became a great person for God after he changed the way he had been living.

- Offer the scripture as a prayer to God:

*Gracious and forgiving God, be with me as I plan this Children's Sermon. Help me to listen to what you would have me say as I talk with the children about your forgiveness, mercy, and love. Open my ears, heart, and mind to the most creative ways in which to work with the children this week. In Jesus' name, Amen.*

- Spend a few minutes in silence, asking God to bless your work in preparation, and to give you any thoughts that would be helpful to you during this time.

## D. Chosen Theme(s)

The themes of Sin, Judgment, and Redemption are important in this portion of Paul's letter, offering an opportunity to talk about this with the children. The children can understand these themes in terms of Sometimes I do wrong, which hurts others; what I do really does matter to God and to me; and God loves me even when I do wrong.

## E. Materials Needed

- Bible
- Letter (written on 8.5 X 11 paper, then rolled up like a scroll, from each side toward the middle; use a rubber band to hold the scroll together until you are ready to unroll it and read it to the children), with the following message on it:

*Dear God,*

*I am very sorry that I harmed some of your Christian men and women. Please forgive me. Thank you for letting me be one of your missionaries to tell others about your love and your son, Jesus Christ.*

*Always your servant,*
*Paul*

- I'm Sorry, Forgive Me mini-scroll for each child (You may want to recruit extra helpers as you put these together, and as you hand them out during the Children's Sermon).
- Handout for each child

## F. Outline

- Invite the children to come forward; greet them with hospitality
- Show them the large scroll; tell a brief story of Paul: Paul was afraid of the early Christians who lived long ago; Paul hurt a lot of them and tried to destroy their churches. Then Paul heard the voice of Jesus, who told Paul to stop hurting the followers of Jesus; Paul asked God to forgive him, and God forgave Paul. Paul went around telling many people about God and wrote a lot of letters to those early churches, the letters we have in our Bibles, like Galatians read today
- Tell the children you've got something that is what Paul's letter might have looked like long ago (only this one is a letter he might have prayed to God; read the letter).

- Give each child their miniature scroll; tell them that the prayer they will say today are the same words on their scrolls. Pray.
- Give out regular handout as well as the miniature scroll.

### G. Handout Suggestion

Summary phrase: "Paul asked God to forgive him." Picture of man praying or of Paul on road to Damascus. This is in addition to the miniature scroll you will give out.

### H. Index Card

- Invite children forward; greet them
- Tell story of Paul
- Show large scroll; read it; pass it around
- Give them their small scrolls
- Lead them in prayer (which is on their scrolls):

  *God, I am sorry when*
  *I do something*
  *that is wrong.*
  *Please forgive me.*
  *I know that you love me.*
  *And I love you.*
  *In Jesus' name we pray. Amen.*

- Give out regular handouts


## YEAR C, PROPER 19

### A. Scriptures

Jeremiah 4:11–12, 22–28; Psalm 14; 1 Timothy 1:12–17; Luke 15:1–10

### B. Process of Selection

Read each of the four scriptures slowly and ask God to help you choose which one of these would work well as the basis for a Children's Sermon.

With your experience you are ready to read each scripture slowly and discern through prayer which one or two scriptures might lend themselves very well for the basis of the Children's Sermon.

Jeremiah 4:11–12 and 22–28 were written at a bleak time in the history of Jerusalem and Judah, and they tell of that bleakness. I would recommend that they not be used with children.

Psalm 14, a psalm denouncing Godlessness in the world, is one of the more negative psalms in our Bible. I would also recommend that this scripture not be used with children.

1 Timothy 1:12–17 are words of thankfulness to God for rescuing a person who had done violence in his former life, but had since been strengthened through a relationship with Jesus Christ. If this scripture is used, either verse 1 or 17 could be used as a doxology type of lesson. This might also be a good time to introduce children of young ages to the "Doxology" if it is sung each week in your worship service. (Often this is sung in the service after children have left for nursery care or extended session or children's worship time). You will want to recruit some help beforehand from the music director, organist, accompanist, or other musical person in your congregation.

Luke 15:1–10 tells the familiar stories of the lost sheep and the lost coin. Either of these would provide an excellent basis for the Children's Sermon.

After reading the above four scriptures for the first Sunday in Lent, I chose the Luke passage. However, you know the children in your church better than I. You may decide that the Timothy scripture and learning about the "Doxology" would provide a good learning opportunity for your group.

Read your chosen scripture again, slowly.

1 Now all the tax-collectors and sinners were coming near to listen to him. 2 And the Pharisees and the scribes were grumbling and saying, "This fellow welcomes sinners and eats with them." 3 So he told them this parable: 4 "Which one of you, having a hundred sheep and losing one of them, does not leave the ninety-nine in the wilderness and go after the one that is lost until he finds it? 5 When he has found it, he lays it on his shoulders and rejoices. 6 And when he comes home, he calls together his friends and neighbours, saying to them, 'Rejoice with me, for I have found my sheep that was lost.' 7 Just so, I tell you, there will be more joy in heaven over one sinner who repents than over ninety-nine righteous people who need no repentance. 8 Or what woman having ten silver coins, if she loses one of them, does not light a lamp, sweep the house, and search carefully until she finds it? 9 When she has found it, she calls together her friends and neighbours, saying, 'Rejoice with me, for I have found the coin that I had lost.' 10 Just so, I tell you, there is joy

in the presence of the angels of God over one sinner who repents." (Lk. 15:1–10)

What are the themes for children in this passage?

*God's Self-Revelation:* Through Jesus, God revealed to the common people that all persons are important to God, even sinners. Especially sinners. Children understand this theme as "God and Jesus love me very much."

*Redemption:* God is always looking for ways to bring the "sinner" or "one who strays" back into the fold. Jesus demonstrated that very well in his stories about the lost sheep and the lost coin. Children relate to this theme when they realize God loves them when they do the right thing and when they make mistakes and do something they should not do.

*Faith-Response:* In both of these parables the person who lost something responded with joy after finding the lost sheep or lost coin. Children also express joy when something good happens to them; they know how to give thanks to God, especially as they pray each week at the end of the Children's Sermon. (You will note that many of the prayers in this book begin with "Thank you, God." If we teach no other prayer to the children in our midst, teaching them to pray, "thank you, God," will be sufficient.)

All of the verses in the Luke scripture (both parables) could be meaningful for the children.

What are the most effective learning methods that could be used with this passage?

- Listening
- Seeing
- Retelling the story
- Experiencing actions through pantomime

### C. Immersing in the Chosen Scripture

- Read the Luke passage again, silently, lingering on the words you know that most of the children will be able to understand. What ideas or concepts might be strange to them? If you live in the city, children may not be very familiar with sheep or with shepherds. "Lighting a lamp" might also need to be explained.
- Read the scripture aloud, slowly, at least two times. As you read the scripture the first time, picture the actual events of

each parable. What do you see happening? What do you hear? What do you smell? Are there any tastes in the parables, e.g., maybe the food that each person shares when they rejoice with their friends and neighbors? Next, read it and think how you might tell it as an "Echo Pantomime," where you will say a phrase and do some motions, and the children will repeat what you say and what you do (to the best of their abilities for their age levels).

- Reflect on this passage; then write down any thoughts, questions, or ideas you might have. Do not neglect this step.
- Offer the scripture as a prayer to God:

*Thank you, God, for these beautiful parables of people who lost and then found something. We are blessed to know that Jesus told them so that we would be assured that you love us so very much that you will continue to seek us when we go astray. Thank you, God, for that kind of love! In the name of your precious son, Jesus, Amen.*

- Spend a few minutes in silence, asking God to bless your work in preparation, and to give you any thoughts that would be helpful to you during this time.

### D. Theme(s)

- *God's Self-Revelation,*
- *Redemption*
- *Faith-Response*
- Chosen Theme: I shall use the theme of *Faith-Response* to develop the Echo Pantomime to use with the children.

### E. Materials Needed

- Bible
- Computer paper or cardstock on which to list your cues for telling the Echo Pantomime. (See content below.)

### F. Outline

- Invite the children forward; greet them with hospitality;
- Explain that you and they will be doing an "Echo Pantomime" where they are to say and do what you say and do. Invite them to stand up and spread out so they have a little room.
- Echo Pantomime:
  1. Once there was a woman (use hands to indicate long, flowing hair)
  2. who had ten silver coins (count them on your fingers)

3. One day she could find only nine coins (count to nine on fingers two times; look puzzled as you look around you);
4. So she got her broom and began to sweep the floor (pantomime sweeping);
5. She swept in the corners (sweep in imaginary corners);
6. She got down on her knees to look under the bed (get down and look);
7. She was so sad to have lost one of her ten coins (sad face);
8. But suddenly she saw the coin (point and look excited, clap your hands)!
9. She was so happy, she shared her joy with her friends (join hands and swing your arms up and down together).

- Tell the children, "And God loves us much more than that woman loved her coins. That's why God gets so excited when we come to church to learn about Jesus and God and the stories in the Bible.
- Give children handouts and pray.

### G. Handout Suggestion

Summary phrase: "Rejoice with me, for I have found the coin that I had lost." Show picture of woman sweeping, perhaps picture of coin.

### H. Index Card

- Invite the children forward; greet them
- Explain "Echo Pantomime"
- Do "Echo Pantomime" (perhaps print story and actions on flip side of index card)
- Say: "God loves us much more than that woman loved her coins. That's why God gets so excited when we come to church to learn about Jesus and God and the stories in the Bible."
- Give children handouts and pray:

  *Thank you, dear God,*
  *for your wonderful love!*
  *Thank you for the stories*
  *Jesus told long ago.*
  *They remind us that*
  *we are your children!*
  *In Jesus' name we pray, Amen.*

CHAPTER NINE

# Sample Children's Sermons, Lectionary Year A

## YEAR A, ADVENT 3

### A. Scriptures

Isaiah 35:1–10; Psalm 146:5–10; James 5:7–10; Matthew 11:2–11; Luke 1:46–55

### B. Process of Selection

Read each scripture selection carefully, asking God to open your eyes, mind, and heart as to which ones would work well as the basis for a Children's Sermon.

### 1. Isaiah 35:1–10

1  The wilderness and the dry land shall be glad,
    the desert shall rejoice and blossom;
    like the crocus 2 it shall blossom abundantly,
    and rejoice with joy and singing.
    The glory of Lebanon shall be given to it,
    the majesty of Carmel and Sharon.
    They shall see the glory of the LORD,
    the majesty of our God.
3  Strengthen the weak hands,
    and make firm the feeble knees.
4  Say to those who are of a fearful heart,
    "Be strong, do not fear!
    Here is your God.

> He will come with vengeance,
> with terrible recompense.
> He will come and save you."

5  Then the eyes of the blind shall be opened,
>    and the ears of the deaf unstopped;
6  then the lame shall leap like a deer,
>    and the tongue of the speechless sing for joy.
> For waters shall break forth in the wilderness,
>    and streams in the desert;
7  the burning sand shall become a pool,
>    and the thirsty ground springs of water;
> the haunt of jackals shall become a swamp,
>    the grass shall become reeds and rushes.
8  A highway shall be there,
>    and it shall be called the Holy Way;
> the unclean shall not travel on it,
>    but it shall be for God's people;
>    no traveler, not even fools, shall go astray.
9  No lion shall be there,
>    nor shall any ravenous beast come up on it;
> they shall not be found there,
>    but the redeemed shall walk there.
10  And the ransomed of the LORD shall return,
>    and come to Zion with singing;
> everlasting joy shall be upon their heads;
>    they shall obtain joy and gladness,
>    and sorrow and sighing shall flee away.

In this scripture, verses 1–2 or 5–7 could work well as the basis of a Children's Sermon.

**Themes for these five verses would include:**

*Creation:* God made the wilderness, the dry land, the blossoming desert, the crocus, and all the people who dwell therein. God also made all persons, with all their varying characteristics, limitations, and challenges. Everything that we find in the created world, God created. For children this theme is understood best by the phrases "God made me; God made everything."

*Providence:* Children understand the theme of providence through recognition that God plans for a good world, and God wants to help us. In the five verses from the book of Isaiah, it is apparent that God does plan for a good world through sending rain when it is needed, and blossoms, and a cause for people to rejoice. Verses 5 through 7 stress the plans that God has for all people: the blind shall see, the deaf shall hear, the lame shall walk and leap, and the mute shall be able to speak and sing. Again, God shall provide water and growth to the desert areas.

*Hope:* A child's hope in God, of course, depends on a child's experience with the adults in his or her life. A child whose parents keep their promises also sees God as One who keeps promises. The child has hope that God will always take care of him or her, if the parent figures for that child provide adequate and consistent care.

**One way to develop this scripture into the Children's Sermon:** Since the themes of the scripture deal with creation, providence, and hope, bringing in a growing plant might be a way to begin. (And this would work especially well with the James passage). A very small tree would be ideal. A person who plants a tree is usually thinking into the future, probably many years. Sometimes we do not get to see the results of planting a tree, at least not the fully grown tree. Planting a seedling tree involves much hope: hope that the tree will continue to thrive and hope that our children and/ or our grandchildren will be able to someday enjoy the shade of that tree (or its fruit).

• • • • • • •

### 2. Psalm 146:5–10

5  Happy are those whose help is the God of Jacob,
      whose hope is in the LORD their God,
6  who made heaven and earth,
      the sea, and all that is in them;
   who keeps faith forever;
7  who executes justice for the oppressed;
      who gives food to the hungry.

   The LORD sets the prisoners free;
8     the LORD opens the eyes of the blind.
   The LORD lifts up those who are bowed down;
      the LORD loves the righteous.
9  The LORD watches over the strangers;
      he upholds the orphan and the widow,
      but the way of the wicked he brings to ruin.

10    The LORD will reign forever,
        your God, O Zion, for all generations.
      Praise the LORD!

In this scripture, all of the verses (with the possible exception of verse 9c, "but the way of the wicked he brings to ruin,") would be usable as the basis for the Children's Sermon.

**Themes in children's terms for Psalm 146:5–10 include:**

*Faith-Response:* As the People of God, our response to God's many blessings is to feel happiness. Children's understanding of this theme is, "I am happy!"

*Hope:* We can have hope that all of the promises listed in this psalm will come or are coming true.

*Creation:* God has made heaven and earth and the sea and "all that is in them." Children also understand that God has created them.

*Providence:* In this psalm God provides justice, freedom, food, sight, and watchfulness. God plans for a good world, and God does help each of us in many ways.

*Judgment:* What we do really does matter, and part of who we are is to be helpers in doing some of the things which God is shown to do in this psalm.

*Sin/Redemption:* We will make mistakes at times, but God continues to love us. Even when we do wrong.

**One way to develop this scripture into the Children's Sermon:** Choose one of the verses or phrases to emphasize, such as, The LORD lifts up those who are bowed down. Talk about that theme with the children. What does it mean to be bowed down? Some children may think this means "to bow down," as in to kneel. You would need to explain that being bowed down is to feel "weighted down" with some kind of sorrow or worry or difficult situation. Guide the children in seeing some of the things God provides for us when we are bowed down: friends and family who love us; a church where we can pray and sing together; ministers and teachers who will listen to us and help us find solutions to our problems; and a God who loves us more than we've ever been loved before.

· · · · · · ·

### 3. James 5:7–10

7 Be patient, therefore, beloved, until the coming of the Lord. The farmer waits for the precious crop from the earth,

being patient with it until it receives the early and the late rains. 8 You also must be patient. Strengthen your hearts, for the coming of the Lord is near. 9 Beloved, do not grumble against one another, so that you may not be judged. See, the Judge is standing at the doors! 10 As an example of suffering and patience, beloved, take the prophets who spoke in the name of the Lord.

In this scripture, verse 7 could possibly work well as a basis for the Children's Sermon, particularly if you tied in the theme of patience while growing plants, and patience while waiting for Christmas during the season of Advent.

**Themes in children's terms for this scripture include:**

*Providence:* God plans for a good world. However, many of the good things of God come in God's timing, which is not always our timing. James 5:7 reminds us of this, "Be patient, therefore, beloved, until the coming of the Lord." Patience can be very difficult for children around the Christmas season. Advent can seem like a long delay. Part of being the People of God is to anticipate Christ's coming each year, beginning with the first Sunday in Advent.

*Hope:* Hope is believing that God will always keep God's promises. Several of the scriptures for Advent 3, Year A, have a theme of hope in them. Advent is very much the season of hope, in addition to the season of waiting. We wait because we do hope. Even young children can begin to talk about what they "hope for" during this season. The James passage looks ahead to the second coming of Jesus Christ, which would be a difficult concept for children. They, do, however, understand the hoping and the waiting during this season of Advent.

*Creation:* As Creator of the world, God made everything. However, God needs God's People to help care for creation. Sometimes that too involves a lot of patience, especially when things do not improve as quickly as we think they should (e.g., trying to improve the environment so that it will be better for future generations).

**One way to develop this scripture into the Children's Sermon:** (See the suggestions under the Isaiah 35 scripture above, which would also work very well with the James scripture, especially as you look at patience; patience is growing a tree, patience is waiting for the Christ Child during the season in Advent.)

• • • • • • •

### 4. Matthew 11:2-11

2 When John heard in prison what the Messiah was doing, he sent word by his disciples 3 and said to him, "Are you the one who is to come, or are we to wait for another?" 4 Jesus answered them, "Go and tell John what you hear and see: 5 the blind receive their sight, the lame walk, the lepers are cleansed, the deaf hear, the dead are raised, and the poor have good news brought to them. 6 And blessed is anyone who takes no offense at me." 7 As they went away, Jesus began to speak to the crowds about John: "What did you go out into the wilderness to look at? A reed shaken by the wind? 8 What then did you go out to see? Someone dressed in soft robes? Look, those who wear soft robes are in royal palaces. 9 What then did you go out to see? A prophet? Yes, I tell you, and more than a prophet. 10 This is the one about whom it is written,

'See, I am sending my messenger ahead of you,
  who will prepare your way before you.'

11 Truly I tell you, among those born of women no one has arisen greater than John the Baptist; yet the least in the kingdom of heaven is greater than he."

Possible verses/phrases that would work well with the Children's Sermon would be verses 2 and 3, John's sending of his disciples to make sure that he was correct about who Jesus really is, and Jesus' beautiful words of response: "Go and tell John what you hear and see: the blind receive their sight, the lame walk, the lepers are cleansed, the deaf hear, the dead are raised, and the poor have good news brought to them. And blessed is anyone who takes no offense at me."

**Themes:**

*God's Self Revelation:* God revealed God's Self through both John the Baptist and Jesus; God is good; God loves me.

*People of God:* Both John the Baptist and Jesus belonged to the People of God; each of us belongs to the People of God.

*Hope:* through both John the Baptist and Jesus, God was keeping promises made to the Hebrew people long ago; God can be trusted, for God does keep the promises God makes.

**One way to develop this scripture into the Children's Sermon:** Concentrating on John's questions from prison, and Jesus' reply, you could tell the story briefly. You could emphasize that sometimes people do get discouraged when they are in a bad situation such as John the Baptist was in. But Jesus wanted to reassure him, through all that he was doing in God's name (healing and teaching and preaching the Good News) that he, Jesus, was indeed the Son of God, the one whom God had sent to the people.

· · · · · · ·

### 5. Luke 1:46–55 (46–55)

46     And Mary said,
        "My soul magnifies the Lord,
47     and my spirit rejoices in God my Savior,
48     for he has looked with favor on the lowliness of his servant.
        Surely, from now on all generations will call me blessed;
49     for the Mighty One has done great things for me,
        and holy is his name.
50     His mercy is for those who fear him
        from generation to generation.
51     He has shown strength with his arm;
        he has scattered the proud in the thoughts of their hearts.
52     He has brought down the powerful from their thrones,
        and lifted up the lowly;
53     he has filled the hungry with good things,
        and sent the rich away empty.
54     He has helped his servant Israel,
        in remembrance of his mercy,
55     according to the promise he made to our ancestors,
        to Abraham and to his descendants forever."

Some important verses to which children would relate are 46–48; 49–50; 53a, and 55.

#### Themes:

*Faith-Response:* Mary responded in faith to the angel's message, and magnified (or gave glory to) God. She was saying, "Thank you, God; I love you, God."

*Self-Revelation:* God had revealed a great plan, which involved Mary and the birth of God's Son, Jesus. God's plan was great. God is good; God loves me.

**One way to develop this scripture into the Children's Sermon:** Verse 46 would be a good starting place for talking about what it means to "magnify" something or somebody. And then, try to understand why Mary was "magnifying" God.

This is the scripture I chose for this particular week.

· · · · · · ·

## C. Immersing in the Chosen Scripture

- Read silently, again, Luke 1:46–55.
- Read the scripture aloud, slowly, at least two times. *The first time* you read it, put yourself in Mary's place: a young girl who has just heard unbelievable, extraordinary news. Imagine all of the doubts and fears you might experience at the strange news the angel told you (Lk. 1:26–34). *The second time* you read it, read it with the assurance that Mary heard from the angel (Lk. 1:35–45), and the assurance you find in her words in our passage. Look carefully for the accepting and excited attitude on her part. What made the difference in Mary's feelings and attitude? Where do you need and want her kind of confidence in God in your life?
- Reflect on this passage, then write down any thoughts, questions, or ideas you might have.
- Which verses/verse do you think would be most appropriate for a Children's Sermon?
- Offer the scripture as a prayer to God:

  *Thank you, God, for the faith that we find in Mary. What a role model she can be to us today! Give me faith in your blessings as I prepare the Children's Sermon. Fill me with your ideas and picture in my mind the faces of the children who will be coming forward this week. In Jesus' name, Amen.*

- Spend a few minutes in silence, asking God to bless your work in this preparation, and to give you any thoughts that would be helpful to you during this time.

## D. Theme(s)

Faith-Response:

We shall explore with the children what it means to respond to God's love and the Good News of Jesus Christ as faithful followers.

## E. Materials Needed

- Bible, with this passage marked
- a magnifying glass
- a picture of the Annunciation (check Sunday school curriculum pictures; art books, see appendix B for possibilities)
- a handout for each child

### F. Outline

- Invite the children forward; greet them with hospitality
- Show the children the magnifying glass
- Ask them what it is and what it does
- Show a picture of the angel appearing to Mary (the annunciation)
- Read Luke 1:46–47 aloud to the children
- Explain that *magnify* does mean to make larger, but it also means to praise greatly. Explain why Mary praised God (God had kept a promise to send a Savior)
- Give each child a handout and pray.

### G. Handout Suggestion

Summary phrase: "My soul magnifies the Lord, and my spirit rejoices in God." Picture of annunciation.

### I. Index Card

- Invite children forward; greet them
- Show magnifying glass; What is it? What does it do?
- Show annunciation picture
- Read Luke 1:46–47
- Meanings of *magnify*
- Why Mary magnified God
- Give children the handouts and pray:

  *Thank you, God, for Mary.*
  *Thank you for her praises of You.*
  *Teach us how to praise You*
  *for the wonderful things*
  *You do every day.*
  *In Jesus' name we pray, Amen.*

## YEAR A, Epiphany

### A. Scriptures

Isaiah 60:1–6; Psalm 72:1–7, 10–14; Ephesians 3:1–12; Matthew 2:1–12

### B. Process of Selection

Read each scripture selection carefully, asking God to open your eyes, mind, and heart as to which one would work well as the basis for a Children's Sermon.

## 1. Isaiah 60:1–6

1  Arise, shine; for your light has come,
      and the glory of the LORD has risen upon you.
2  For darkness shall cover the earth,
      and thick darkness the peoples;
   but the LORD will arise upon you,
      and his glory will appear over you.
3  Nations shall come to your light,
      and kings to the brightness of your dawn.
4  Lift up your eyes and look around;
      they all gather together, they come to you;
   your sons shall come from far away,
      and your daughters shall be carried on their nurses' arms.
5  Then you shall see and be radiant;
      your heart shall thrill and rejoice,
   because the abundance of the sea shall be brought to you,
      the wealth of the nations shall come to you.
6  A multitude of camels shall cover you,
      the young camels of Midian and Ephah;
   all those from Sheba shall come.
   They shall bring gold and frankincense,
      and shall proclaim the praise of the LORD.

The Isaiah passage includes several verses, or phrases, that would work well with the Children's Sermon: verses 1, 2c-d, 3, and 5.

If I were to use this scripture, I would probably concentrate on verse 1: "Arise, shine; for your light has come, and the glory of the LORD has risen upon you." We celebrate Epiphany and the Season of Epiphany as the Season of Light. We look at the many ways in which God's "Light" has broken forth into our world. This is the season in which we celebrate the coming of the Magi, bearing gifts from far lands. God's Light broke into their lives as they followed the star to Bethlehem. We also read some of the scriptures surrounding Jesus and the light in his life: his baptism, in which God spoke words to him and a dove descended upon him; his first miracle at a wedding feast in Cana. All of these stories have to do with God's Light.

### Themes:

*Creation:* God made everything, including light, Baby Jesus, and the Magi (the kings from afar).

*People of God:* Each of us belongs to God's family; we are part of the Church; we celebrate the season of Epiphany as a Church family.

*Providence:* God plans for a good world; God helps us; through Jesus, God has provided a special way to draw closer to God.

*Hope:* God made a promise to the Hebrew people, such as found in the scripture in Isaiah 60; God always keeps God's promises.

**One way of developing the Isaiah scripture:** Have several different kinds of light for the children to see, handle, and talk about. (From candles to flashlight to a small reading light, with, perhaps, at least one of them connected to a source of electricity so you can turn it on at the proper time). All these different kinds of lights are gifts from God, even the invention of the light bulb. God created the people who invented the various forms of light bulbs and gave them the necessary knowledge and perseverance to create light for us. Ask the children to name some things they could not do as well if we did not have sources of light (and you could include the sun in this list). You could close with a prayer of thanksgiving for the ways in which God has provided light for us.

### 2. Psalm 72:1–7, 10–14

1   Give the king your justice, O God,
      and your righteousness to a king's son.
2   May he judge your people with righteousness,
      and your poor with justice.
3   May the mountains yield prosperity for the people,
      and the hills, in righteousness.
4   May he defend the cause of the poor of the people,
      give deliverance to the needy,
      and crush the oppressor.
5   May he live while the sun endures,
      and as long as the moon, throughout all generations.
6   May he be like rain that falls on the mown grass,
      like showers that water the earth.
7   In his days may righteousness flourish
      and peace abound, until the moon is no more...
10   May the kings of Tarshish and of the isles
        render him tribute,
      may the kings of Sheba and Seba
        bring gifts.
11   May all kings fall down before him,
        all nations give him service.
12   For he delivers the needy when they call,
        the poor and those who have no helper.

13    He has pity on the weak and the needy,
         and saves the lives of the needy.
14    From oppression and violence he redeems their life;
         and precious is their blood in his sight.

This psalm is one in which the people are praying to God, asking God to watch over their king. I would recommend not using this scripture since we are not ruled by kings. And for many in the church, trying to adapt this psalm for a president or high-ranking, secular official would not be appropriate. There are more suitable scripture passages for this day that could be used very successfully in a good Children's Sermon.

• • • • • • •

### 3. Ephesians 3:1–12

1 This is the reason that I Paul am a prisoner for Christ Jesus for the sake of you Gentiles–2 for surely you have already heard of the commission of God's grace that was given me for you, 3 and how the mystery was made known to me by revelation, as I wrote above in a few words, 4 a reading of which will enable you to perceive my understanding of the mystery of Christ. 5 In former generations this mystery was not made known to humankind, as it has now been revealed to his holy apostles and prophets by the Spirit: 6 that is, the Gentiles have become fellow heirs, members of the same body, and sharers in the promise in Christ Jesus through the gospel. 7 Of this gospel I have become a servant according to the gift of God's grace that was given me by the working of his power. 8 Although I am the very least of all the saints, this grace was given to me to bring to the Gentiles the news of the boundless riches of Christ, 9 and to make everyone see what is the plan of the mystery hidden for ages in God who created all things; 10 so that through the church the wisdom of God in its rich variety might now be made known to the rulers and authorities in the heavenly places. 11 This was in accordance with the eternal purpose that he has carried out in Christ Jesus our Lord, 12 in whom we have access to God in boldness and confidence through faith in him.

**Themes in children's terms for the Ephesians passage:**

*Providence:* Even though Paul is in prison, he still knows that God is taking care of him; Paul believed that God did plan for a good world and that God would help him no matter what happened. God cares for us when we are going through tough times.

*Creation:* In verse 9, Paul praises God *who created all things.* That includes the Church, which helps others to understand the love of God.

*Hope:* Paul's hope was in the gift of Jesus Christ, who helped him understand God and brought him closer to God.

*God's Self-Revelation:* Paul did not know Jesus before the resurrection, but he believed that God sent Jesus to talk with him after Jesus' resurrection. Jesus talked with Paul, and Paul changed his ways; he became a follower of Jesus.

**One way of developing the Ephesians scripture:** Tell the story of Paul briefly and stress how he continued to trust God through his hard times. You could ask the children if they know anyone who is struggling through hard times. Be ready to provide an example (using someone you know, without mentioning any names, who is very unlikely to be known in the church). Have the children suggest ways that you might help this person know that God still loves her or him; and ways that you might share this love. A possible handout would be to create a card that would have an "all-purpose" theme, such as, "God loves you, and so do I!" (Or, "and so do we!")

• • • • • • •

### 4. Matthew 2:1-12

1 In the time of King Herod, after Jesus was born in Bethlehem of Judea, wise men from the East came to Jerusalem, 2 asking, "Where is the child who has been born king of the Jews? For we observed his star at its rising, and have come to pay him homage." 3 When King Herod heard this, he was frightened, and all Jerusalem with him; 4 and calling together all the chief priests and scribes of the people, he inquired of them where the Messiah was to be born. 5 They told him, "In Bethlehem of Judea; for so it has been written by the prophet:

6 'And you, Bethlehem, in the land of Judah,
    are by no means least among the rulers of Judah;
for from you shall come a ruler
    who is to shepherd my people Israel.'"

7 Then Herod secretly called for the wise men and learned from them the exact time when the star had appeared. 8 Then he sent them to Bethlehem, saying, "Go and search diligently

for the child; and when you have found him, bring me word so that I may also go and pay him homage." 9 When they had heard the king, they set out; and there, ahead of them, went the star that they had seen at its rising, until it stopped over the place where the child was. 10 When they saw that the star had stopped, they were overwhelmed with joy. 11 On entering the house, they saw the child with Mary his mother; and they knelt down and paid him homage. Then, opening their treasure chests, they offered him gifts of gold, frankincense, and myrrh. 12 And having been warned in a dream not to return to Herod, they left for their own country by another road.

The passage from Matthew has the most potential for providing an interesting and memorable scripture for this particular Sunday, Epiphany.

**Themes in children's terms for this passage:**

*Hope:* God always keeps God's promises; God promised a Savior to the Hebrew people long before Jesus was born, and God kept that promise, as reported in this scripture passage.

*People of God:* The People of God in the Matthew passage also included the kings who came from the Far East to bring gifts to the Christ child; God's People include people all over the world; each of us is part of the family of God.

*Providence:* God plans for a good world; in the above scripture, God's plan included a dream for the kings from the Far East so that they would not return to King Herod, who was trying to get rid of baby Jesus.

### C. Immersing in the Chosen Scripture

- Read silently, again, Matthew 2:1–12.
- Read the scripture aloud, slowly, at least two times. *The first time*, picture yourself in each scene of the story: traveling with the wise men and stopping to inquire of King Herod; being present in King Herod's court as he gathered the wisest persons in his kingdom; the wise men talking with Herod before they traveled on; their arrival at the stable/manger in Bethlehem and going into the area where baby Jesus and his parents were; and the wise men talking together after one of them had a dream from God. *The second time* you read the passage, put yourself in

the place of a wise man who was not a Jew and would look at the scene with wonderment and suspicion as they followed the star. What would be your comments about each of the scenes? What would you be thinking, feeling, saying?

- Reflect on this passage; then write down any thoughts, questions, or ideas you might have. Which of the story parts would be difficult for the children to understand? Why would this be? What can you do to prepare your time with them so that they will be better able to understand this special passage?

- Which verses/verse do you think would be most appropriate for a Children's Sermon? Because you know your children better than I (and if you do not feel like you know them, please go back and reread chapter 2, "How Well Do You Know Your Audience?"), you may, at times, choose to do something very different from what I have outlined. If it is bringing the children closer to God in positive, affirming ways, then trust your own instincts. I would choose the kings' arrival at the manger and the gift-giving portion, verses 9–12, but I would tie these in with the theme of *Hope*, particularly as it relates to *God's Promises.*

- Offer the scripture as a prayer to God:

  *Thank you, God, for the privilege of working with the children in our church. Place on my heart the kind of love that you and Jesus have for children. Open my eyes and my mind to what you would have me say and do with these little ones. Help our time together be a wonderful time in which they feel your presence very close to them. In Jesus' name I pray, Amen.*

- Spend a few minutes in silence, asking God to bless your work in preparation, and to give you any thoughts that would be helpful to you during this time.

What are the most effective learning methods that could be used with this scripture?

- *Listening,* they hear about God's faithfulness in keeping promises,
- *Responding,* as the children share how persons in their lives have kept promises to them and how they keep promises they make to other people;
- *Touching,* as they handle a beautifully wrapped box.

**One way to develop this scripture into the Children's Sermon:** Using verses 9–12, I would tell a brief story of God promising the Hebrew people, long ago, a Savior. God kept that promise by sending baby Jesus into the world. The wise men who followed the bright star to the manger brought gifts to baby Jesus because they knew he was sent from God. God spoke to the wise men, in a dream, and told them to go home another way so that the wicked king, Herod, could not find Jesus. All these things happened to help make God's promise to the Hebrew people come true.

Next, we would talk about promises. What is a promise? Has someone ever made a promise to you and kept it? How did you feel? Have you ever made a promise to someone and kept that promise? How did you feel? (Keeping promises is part of God's good plan. God kept God's promises first, then people would learn to keep their promises.)

### D. Theme

*Hope.* We shall explore what it means to make and to keep promises.

### E. Materials Needed

- Bible, with the Matthew 2 passage marked
- beautifully wrapped box, or a very fancy box with a ribbon (reminder of Magi)
- a handout for each child to take home

### F. Outline

- Invite the children forward; greet them as they sit around you
- Show them the beautiful present; explain that the kings from the East brought special gifts to Jesus at his birth; this gift is a reminder of that; pass it around for the children to touch.
- Talk with them about promises, beginning with the wonderful promise God made to the Hebrew people long, long ago.
- Questions: Has someone ever made a promise to you and then kept it? How did that make you feel? Have you ever made a promise to someone and then kept it? How did *that* make you feel?
- Two things happened in this story so that God's promise to the Hebrew people of a special Savior (the baby Jesus) could come true: (1) God warned the wise men, in a dream, to not

go back to see the wicked King Herod on their way home; and (2) the wise men listened to and obeyed the dream.
- God showed us how important it is to keep promises we make to other people.
- Give children handouts and pray.

### G. Handout Suggestion

Summary phrase: "God keeps promises. So should we." Show pictures of the wise men, their gifts, the star, etc.

### I. Index Card
- Invite the children forward; greet them
- Pass around and explain beautiful present;
- Talk about promises.
- Ask: Has someone ever made a promise to you and then kept it? How did that make you feel? Have you ever made a promise to someone and then kept it? How did *that* make you feel?
- Review what happened in story.
- Give children  handouts and pray:

  *Thank you, God,*
  *for keeping your promise*
  *of sending a Savior,*
  *Baby Jesus.*
  *Thank you for the wise men*
  *who listened to you.*
  *Help us to keep our promises.*
  *In Jesus' name we pray. Amen.*

### YEAR A, LENT 1

### A. Scriptures

Genesis 2:15–17; 3:1–7; Psalm 32; Romans 5:12–19; Matthew 4:1–11

### B. Process of Selection

Read each of the four scriptures slowly, and ask God to help you choose which one of these would work well as the basis for a Children's Sermon.

Having some experience, you can read each scripture slowly and discern through prayer which one or two scriptures might lend themselves very well for the basis of the Children's Sermon.

After reading the above four scriptures for the first Sunday in Lent, I chose Psalm 32 as the one I would be using for the Children's Sermon (this happened to be the one I was using for my sermon that day).

Read your chosen scripture again, slowly.

1   Happy are those whose transgression is forgiven,
     whose sin is covered.
2   Happy are those to whom the LORD imputes no iniquity,
     and in whose spirit there is no deceit.
3   While I kept silence, my body wasted away
     through my groaning all day long.
4   For day and night your hand was heavy upon me;
     my strength was dried up as by the heat of summer.
5   Then I acknowledged my sin to you,
     and I did not hide my iniquity;
   I said, "I will confess my transgressions to the LORD,"
     and you forgave the guilt of my sin.
6   Therefore let all who are faithful
     offer prayer to you;
   at a time of distress, the rush of mighty waters
     shall not reach them.
7   You are a hiding place for me;
     you preserve me from trouble;
     you surround me with glad cries of deliverance.
8   I will instruct you and teach you the way you should go;
     I will counsel you with my eye upon you.
9   Do not be like a horse or a mule, without understanding,
     whose temper must be curbed with bit and bridle,
   else it will not stay near you.
10   Many are the torments of the wicked,
     but steadfast love surrounds those who trust in the LORD.
11   Be glad in the LORD and rejoice, O righteous,
     and shout for joy, all you upright in heart.

What are the themes for children in this passage?

*Redemption:* Children understand this theme as God loves me all the time, even when I do wrong; God loves me when I'm good and when I'm not good.

*Sin:* When I do wrong, I disappoint God, others, and myself. Doing wrong hurts me, and it hurts others.

*Judgment:* What we do really does matter–to God, to others, and to myself. We must live with the outcomes of our poor choices; God gives us the freedom to make choices.

*Providence:* God will continue to care for me, at all times; God plans for a good world; God helps us as we live out our lives in this world.

*God's Self-Revelation:* God wants to teach us the ways in which we should live.

What verses are especially meaningful for children? Because I was using the topic of "Forgiveness" on this Sunday, verses 5c–7 in Psalm 32 would be especially meaningful to the children.

What are the most effective learning methods that could be used with this passage?

- Listening and Responding
- Retelling the Story, using a picture page
- Experiencing an Occasion of asking forgiveness

### C. Immersing in the Chosen Scripture

- Read Psalm 32 again, silently, lingering on the words that you know that most of the children will be able to understand. What words might be more difficult for them? Explaining that *transgressions* and *iniquities* are other ways to say *sins* will help the children to better understand this psalm.
- Read the scripture aloud, slowly, at least two times. As you read the scripture *the first time,* place yourself in the story as the psalmist. What have you done that has alienated you from God? (In your own mind; we usually *alienate ourselves.*) How do you feel, in your heart and in your mind, knowing that God's hand was "heavy upon you?" Next, read this passage and concentrate on verses 8 through 11. How does the ending of this psalm help you get through the turmoil of having done something that, in *your* heart, separated you from God? Were you able to feel once again that God loves you and wants to instruct you to do what is pleasing in God's sight? Finally, read it *as one living today,* in the twenty-first century. What kinds of things being done in the world around you might cause someone to feel burdened with their sin? Do you feel burdened with your sin? What can you do about it? How does

this affect the words you will use with the children during the Children's Sermon?

- Reflect on this passage; then write down any thoughts, questions, or ideas that *you might have. Do not neglect this step.*
- Which verses/verse do you think would be most appropriate for a Children's Sermon? You may decide to use ones other than the ones I chose. Always feel free to *do this,* because *you know your group of children better than do I,* their needs, their interests, their capabilities, etc.
- Offer the scripture as a prayer to God:

    *Thank you, God, for your love and blessing in my life. Thank you, especially, for your willingness to forgive me when I do wrong. Please forgive my sins right now. Thank you for the gift of your Son Jesus, who made us realize how very much you want to be a part of our lives. This prayer I ask in his name, Amen.*

- Spend a few minutes in silence, asking God to bless your work in preparation and to give you any thoughts that would be helpful to you during this time.

### D. Theme(s)

Chosen Theme–*Redemption.* I shall use the theme of God's loving us no matter what as we discuss forgiveness in this Children's Sermon during Lent.

### E. Materials Needed

- Bible
- Pictures of the Joseph story (which can be made using The Print Shop Deluxe, and printed onto an 8.5 x 11 sheet of cardstock); or you might find pictures in old curricula or in one of the Children's Bibles (See appendix B, Suggested Books)
- Handout cards for children to keep

### F. Outline

- Invite the children forward; greet them warmly.
- Today we're talking about forgiveness. What does it mean to forgive someone?
- One of the best Bible stories about forgiveness is the story about Joseph, the boy who had the coat of many colors.

- Using the cardstock with the pictures of Joseph and family (or other suggested pictures), let the children help tell the story of Joseph.
- Remind them that forgiveness usually involves two parts: Someone asks to be forgiven; someone forgives the person who asks to be forgiven.
- Encourage the children to ask forgiveness of someone else, if they have hurt that person in any way. Also, encourage them to ask God to help them forgive someone who has done something to them that hurt or embarrassed them.
- Tell the children that you and they will continue to talk about forgiveness from time to time because it is very important, and it is very difficult to do at times.
- Give handouts to the children and pray with them..

### G. Handout Suggestion

Summary phrase: God loves us. God forgives us. God wants us to forgive others." Show picture(s) that represents love, perhaps a heart.

(Note: This Sunday occurred the Sunday before Valentine's Day; I used a heart border, with small heart stickers in various positions on each child's handout.)

### H. Index Card

- Invite the children forward; greet them.
- What does it mean to forgive?
- Story of Joseph using pictures on cards
- Two parts to forgiveness
- Whom do you need to ask for forgiveness? Who do you need to forgive?
- Give handouts to the children and pray:

*Thank you, dear God,*
*for forgiving us*
*when we do something*
*we should not do.*
*Teach us how to forgive others*
*as Jesus forgave others.*
*In Jesus' name we pray. Amen.*

## YEAR A, LENT 3

### A. Scriptures

Exodus 17:1–7; Psalm 95; Romans 5:1–11; John 4:5–42

### B. Process of Selection

Read each of the four scriptures slowly, and ask God to help you choose which one of these would work well as the basis for a Children's Sermon.

With your experience you can read each scripture slowly and discern through prayer which one or two scriptures might lend themselves very well for the basis of the Children's Sermon.

After reading the above four scriptures for the first Sunday in Lent, I chose the John passage, but shortened it for use with the children to John 4:5–26, 28–30.

Read John 4:5–26, 28–30 again, slowly.

5 So he came to a Samaritan city called Sychar, near the plot of ground that Jacob had given to his son Joseph. 6 Jacob's well was there, and Jesus, tired out by his journey, was sitting by the well. It was about noon. 7 A Samaritan woman came to draw water, and Jesus said to her, "Give me a drink." 8 (His disciples had gone to the city to buy food.) 9 The Samaritan woman said to him, "How is it that you, a Jew, ask a drink of me, a woman of Samaria?" (Jews do not share things in common with Samaritans.) 10 Jesus answered her, "If you knew the gift of God, and who it is that is saying to you, 'Give me a drink,' you would have asked him, and he would have given you living water." 11 The woman said to him, "Sir, you have no bucket, and the well is deep. Where do you get that living water? 12 Are you greater than our ancestor Jacob, who gave us the well, and with his sons and his flocks drank from it?" 13 Jesus said to her, "Everyone who drinks of this water will be thirsty again, 14 but those who drink of the water that I will give them will never be thirsty. The water that I will give will become in them a spring of water gushing up to eternal life." 15 The woman said to him, "Sir, give me this water, so that I may never be thirsty or have to keep coming here to draw water." 16 Jesus said to her, "Go, call your husband, and come back." 17 The woman answered him, "I have no husband." Jesus said to her, "You are right in saying, 'I have no husband'; 18 for you have had five husbands, and the one you have now is not your husband. What you have said

is true!" 19 The woman said to him, "Sir, I see that you are
a prophet. 20 Our ancestors worshiped on this mountain,
but you say that the place where people must worship is in
Jerusalem." 21 Jesus said to her, "Woman, believe me, the
hour is coming when you will worship the Father neither on
this mountain nor in Jerusalem. 22 You worship what you
do not know; we worship what we know, for salvation is
from the Jews. 23 But the hour is coming, and is now here,
when the true worshipers will worship the Father in spirit
and truth, for the Father seeks such as these to worship him.
24 God is spirit, and those who worship him must worship
in spirit and truth." 25 The woman said to him, "I know that
Messiah is coming" (who is called Christ). "When he comes,
he will proclaim all things to us." 26 Jesus said to her, "I am
he, the one who is speaking to you." ...28 Then the woman
left her water jar and went back to the city. She said to the
people, 29 "Come and see a man who told me everything
I have ever done! He cannot be the Messiah, can he?" 30
They left the city and were on their way to him.

What are the themes for children in this passage?

*God's Self-Revelation:* God is good; God loves us; Jesus loves us.
Jesus revealed who he was to the Samaritan woman in the story. That
in itself was remarkable because  most of the time Jesus told those
around him, "Do not tell who I am."

*Sin:* Children can understand sin and that this woman was doing
something that she probably should not have done. However, that
would not be the focus of this Children's Sermon. We do not know
the circumstances by which this woman had "many husbands." We
don't need to dwell on that part of the passage.

*Redemption:* In spite of the woman's possible sins, Jesus still talked
with her and shared amazing things with her. By doing this he taught
her of God's love for her all the time, even if and when she might
have sinned.

*People of God:* Several things indicated that this woman was part
of the family of God, not the least of which in later verses Jesus stayed
in her village for "two days."

*Hope:* Jesus helped to fulfill the Samaritan woman's hopes that she
would be able to find the correct "place" in which to worship God.

*Faith-Response:* The Samaritan woman's faith-response was
a beautiful one: she went back and told others about Jesus, the
Messiah!

What verses are especially meaningful for children?

A number of meaningful verses could be used with children: verse 7, in which Jesus asked the Samaritan woman for a drink of water; verse 13, in which Jesus begins to explain the difference between regular water and living water that he can give; verse 26, in which Jesus told the woman that he was the Messiah; and verses 28–30, in which the woman left her water jar, went to tell some of the other villagers about Jesus, and the people came out to see him.

What are the most effective learning methods that could be used with this passage?

- *Seeing and Touching,* through the use of a tangible object, a "water jar"
- *Listening,* as they hear a simple version of the Bible story
- *Acting out,* as one or two children act out the part of the woman leaving her water jar

### C. Immersing in the Chosen Scripture

- Read the John passage again, silently, lingering on the words you know most of the children will be able to understand. Look for words that may be unfamiliar to them. How can you make those words more understandable?
- Read the scripture aloud, slowly, at least two times. Read it *first* from the viewpoint of the Samaritan woman. Put yourself into her sandals; what does she think when she sees this lone man sitting by the well in the middle of the day? What does she feel when she hears him ask her for a drink? How does she react when he tells her to bring her husband, and then can tell her exactly what has been going on in her life? Next, read it from the viewpoint of Jesus, as he contemplates how he shall reach this Samaritan woman and what she and other people might think when they see a Jewish man talking to an unescorted Samaritan woman.
- Reflect on this passage; then write down any thoughts, questions, or ideas you might have. *Do not neglect this step.*
- Which verses/verse do you think would be most appropriate for a Children's Sermon? You will note that I have chosen to use the fact that the woman, in her excitement to tell others about Jesus, left her precious water jar filled with water. You may decide to focus on something different in this story.
- Offer the scripture as a prayer to God:

*Thank you, God, for the story of Jesus talking with the Samaritan woman at the well. Let this be a reminder to me that all people are your children. Help me to always look for opportunities to tell others about you, your love for us, and what you did for us through your son, Jesus Christ, in whose name I pray. Amen.*

- Spend a few minutes in silence, asking God to bless your work in preparation and to give you any thoughts that would be helpful to you during this time.

### D. Theme(s)

Chosen Theme: I shall use the theme of *Faith-Response* as the woman gets so excited about talking with Jesus, the long-awaited Messiah, that she completely forgets to carry her water jar with her back into the village.

### E. Materials Needed

- A large water jar (pottery would be good; inexpensive ones can be found)
- Bible
- Handout cards for children to keep

### F. Outline

- Invite the children forward; greet them cordially.
- Show them the water jar you have brought.
- Tell them a brief version of today's scripture passage: Jesus and his disciples were traveling through Samaria; the disciples went into a nearby village to get food; Jesus sat down beside the village well. A woman came to get water for her family; Jesus asked for a drink. Surprised that this man would talk with her, she got into a conversation with him about religion. She discovered that Jesus knew personal things about her that made her wonder who he was. The woman mentioned something about the Messiah (the savior that God had promised to send to the Jews). Jesus told her that he was the Messiah. The woman got so excited that she hurried back to her village to tell the others about Jesus!
- Ask the children if someone would like to demonstrate how the woman was able to forget her water jar and how she would have walked back to her village (let a couple of children do this, if they choose; otherwise you may want to demonstrate, with one of the children being Jesus).

- Assure the children that it is a good thing to get excited about Jesus and to want to tell others about him.
- Give handouts to children and pray with them.

### G. Handout Suggestion

Summary phrase: "I would have given you living water." Include a picture of Jesus and the woman at the well.

### H. Index Card

- Invite the children forward; greet them
- Show water jar.
- Tell story of Jesus and the woman at the well.
- Demonstrate (you or children) being so excited, you forget your water jar.
- Assure the children that it is a good thing to get excited about Jesus and to want to tell others about him.
- Give handouts to children and pray:

    *Thank you, God, for our Bibles!*
    *Thank you for the people*
    *Who wrote the stories*
    *In the Bible.*
    *Thank you for the woman at the well*
    *Who shared the Good News*
    *With her village.*
    *In Jesus' name we pray, Amen.*

### YEAR A, EASTER

### A. Scriptures

Psalm 118:1–2, 14–24; Jeremiah 31:1–6; Colossians 3:1–4; Matthew 28:1–10

### B. Another Process of Selection

Read each of the four scriptures slowly, and ask God to help you choose which one of these would work well as the basis for a Children's Sermon.

By now you'll be able to discern through prayer which one or two scriptures might lend themselves very well for the basis of the Children's Sermon. After reading the above four scriptures, I chose the Matthew scripture: 28:1–10. Because it is Easter, the most important holy day of Christianity, I would just plan to use a resurrection scripture for the children, even though they (and we adults!) do not fully understand some of the miraculous elements. However, you know your children, your church traditions, and the specifics for what is happening in your congregation on Easter Sunday, so you might choose another scripture to use. Go through the following steps with your alternate scripture.

Read your chosen scripture again, slowly.

1 After the sabbath, as the first day of the week was dawning, Mary Magdalene and the other Mary went to see the tomb. 2 And suddenly there was a great earthquake; for an angel of the Lord, descending from heaven, came and rolled back the stone and sat on it. 3 His appearance was like lightning, and his clothing white as snow. 4 For fear of him the guards shook and became like dead men. 5 But the angel said to the women, "Do not be afraid; I know that you are looking for Jesus who was crucified. 6 He is not here; for he has been raised, as he said. Come, see the place where he lay. 7 Then go quickly and tell his disciples, 'He has been raised from the dead, and indeed he is going ahead of you to Galilee; there you will see him.' This is my message for you." 8 So they left the tomb quickly with fear and great joy, and ran to tell his disciples. 9 Suddenly Jesus met them and said, "Greetings!" And they came to him, took hold of his feet, and worshiped him. 10 Then Jesus said to them, "Do not be afraid; go and tell my brothers to go to Galilee; there they will see me."

What are the themes for children in this passage?

*God's Self-Revelation*: God is good; God revealed God's Self through the voice and instructions of the angel in the tomb.

*People of God*: The women who went to the tomb belonged to the People of God. They were a very important part of the Bible story. Each child belongs to the whole People of God; each one is important to the continuing story.

*Providence*: God does plan for a good world, and Jesus' crucifixion and resurrection were a major part of that good plan.

*Hope*: Because of what God did through Jesus, each of us has hope in our lives. God demonstrated that God is a Promise-Keeper; Jesus promised in many scriptures that he too was a promise and that we are part of that promise.

*Faith-Response*: Thank you, God; I love you, God. In the "rest of the story," the women responded in faith as they followed the instructions Jesus gave to them. They had already responded in faith by going to the tomb in the first place.

What verses are especially meaningful for children?

- verses 2, 3, and 4: The description of the angel and the angel's actions, and the guards' reactions to the angel
- verse 5: The angel's consideration of the women when he said, "Do not be afraid"
- verse 8: The women's immediate, obedient response to the angel's words
- verses 9 and 10: The women's encounter with Jesus himself

What are the most effective learning methods that could be used with this passage?

- *Listening and seeing* as they hear the story told and see a couple of pictures;
- *Experiencing the part of the women* as the children are told to "Go quickly and tell his disciples, 'He has been raised from the dead.'"

### C. Immersing in the Chosen Scripture

- Read the passage from the gospel of Matthew again, silently, lingering on the words that you know that most of the children will be able to understand. With what words and what concepts might the children have difficulty?
- Read the scripture aloud, slowly, at least two times. *Read it first* as an outside observer, looking on. You might be one of the guards, watching from a distance. What do you see that you cannot understand? What makes logical sense to you? What is so "spiritual" that you might not believe it, even if you were there at the time? *Read it a second time,* and place yourself inside one of the characters in this drama: one of the "like dead men" guards who awakens and observes the entire scene, or one of the two Marys listed. Finally, read it *as one living today,* in the twenty-first century. What parts of this Easter resurrection story do most people have difficulty believing? Why do you think that is? What can you say to children so that they will continue to have enthusiasm for the Easter story? In a culture that sometimes seems to reward

sameness, what are the rewards of being different, especially when it comes to being strong in what you believe?
- Reflect on this passage; then write down any thoughts, questions, or ideas that you might have. *Do not neglect this step.*
- Which verses/verse do you think would be most appropriate for a Children's Sermon?
- Offer the scripture as a prayer to God:

  *Thank you, God, for the good plan you have had for us since before we were born. Thank you for Jesus, the one who brought all of this plan into existence. Lead me in my study and in my teaching as I work with your precious children in our church. Give me the spiritual insight I need to teach this lesson. These things I ask in the name of your son, Jesus, Amen.*

- Spend a few minutes in silence, asking God to bless your work in preparation, and to give you any thoughts that would be helpful to you during this time.

### D. Theme(s)

I shall use the themes of *Hope* and *Faith-Response.*

### E. Materials Needed

- Pictures of women at the empty tomb, angel in the tomb; etc. You can find suitable ones in the two Bibles listed in appendix B—*My First Bible* and *The Toddler's Bible*—plus most Sunday school curriculum series will have a suitable picture of the empty tomb
- Bible
- A handout card for each child (and you will want to make extras for guests on Easter Sunday)
- two smaller cards for each child (can be made on computer with labels, such as Avery 8160 Shipping Labels, ten to a page of cardstock) with the words, "Jesus has been raised from the dead! Jesus lives! Hallelujah!"
- Adult and/or youth helpers to hand out the smaller cards and help the younger children distribute their two cards to persons in the congregation.

### F. Outline

- Invite the children forward; greet them
- Show picture of empty tomb. Ask them what is special about this day. What does Easter mean to them?

- Explain that the angel told the women to go and tell the other disciples that Jesus no longer was dead. He had been raised from the dead! Ask the children, "How do you think the women felt about that news?"
- Today you're going to get a chance to share that Good News in our church!
- Show the small shipping labels with the words, "Jesus lives! Hallelujah!" on them. Have the children read the words with you.
- Tell them that after the prayer, each child will get to "go quickly" and share this Good News with two other people in the congregation by giving them one of these little cards.
- Give children their handouts and ask them to pray after you.

### *G. Handout Suggestions:*

Summary phrase: "Then go quickly and tell his disciples, "Jesus has been raised from the dead." Show picture of empty tomb.

Also prepare handouts on labels as suggested with the words, "Jesus lives! Hallelujah!"

### *H. Index Card*

- Invite the children forward; greet them
- Show picture of empty tomb.
- What does Easter mean to you?
- Angel told women to share the news.
- Today you're going to share that Good News in our church!
- Distribute "Good News" handouts to share
- Give regular handouts to children and pray:
  *Thank you, dear God, for Easter!*
  *Thank you for*
  *each person here today.*
  *Help us tell others*
  *about Easter.*
  *In Jesus' name we pray,*
  *Amen.*

### YEAR A, EASTER 5

### *A. Scriptures*

Acts 7:55–60; Psalm 31:1–5, 15–16; 1 Peter 2:2–10; John 14:1–14

### B. Process of Selection:

You are ready to do the quicker form of choosing a scripture. Read each scripture slowly. Discern through prayer which one or two scriptures might lend themselves very well for the basis of the Children's Sermon.

After reading the above four scriptures for the first Sunday in Lent, I chose 1 Peter 2:2–10.

Read your chosen scripture again, slowly.

2 Like newborn infants, long for the pure, spiritual milk, so that by it you may grow into salvation–3 if indeed you have tasted that the Lord is good. 4 Come to him, a living stone, though rejected by mortals yet chosen and precious in God's sight, and 5 like living stones, let yourselves be built into a spiritual house, to be a holy priesthood, to offer spiritual sacrifices acceptable to God through Jesus Christ.6 For it stands in scripture:

"See, I am laying in Zion a stone,
   a cornerstone chosen and precious;
and whoever believes in him will not be put to shame."

7 To you then who believe, he is precious; but for those who do not believe,

"The stone that the builders rejected
   has become the very head of the corner,"

8 and

"A stone that makes them stumble,
   and a rock that makes them fall."

They stumble because they disobey the word, as they were destined to do. 9 But you are a chosen race, a royal priesthood, a holy nation, God's own people, in order that you may proclaim the mighty acts of him who called you out of darkness into his marvelous light.

10 Once you were not a people,
      but now you are God's people;
once you had not received mercy,
      but now you have received mercy.

What are the themes for children in this passage?

*Creation*: God made each of us. Through Jesus and his disciples, we have been named "a chosen race, a royal priesthood, a holy nation, God's own people."

*God's Self-Revelation:* The above passage definitely describes God's love for God's people. Children will know that God loves them when they realize that they have been called a royal priesthood and God's own people.

*People of God:* This scripture actually states, "but now you are God's people." Children will know that they have been named as belonging to the People of God, which also makes them a part of God's Church.

*Faith-Response:* We will use faith-response with the children when we talk about the kinds of responsibilities that royalty have toward their subjects, just because they are royalty.

What verses are especially meaningful for children?

Portions of verses 9 and 10 would be most suitable to use with young children: "you are a chosen race, a royal priesthood, a holy nation, God's own people;' "you may proclaim the mighty acts of him who called you;" "but now you are God's people."

What are the most effective learning methods that could be used with this passage?

* *Seeing and listening,* as they see some pictures of modern-day royalty and hear something about each of the royal people;
* *Seeing, listening, and self-examination,* as each child gets to look in a mirror while you direct them in their thinking about who they are.

### C. Immersing in the Chosen Scripture:

- Read the 1 Peter passage again, silently, lingering on the words that you know that most of the children will be able to understand. Concentrate especially on verses 9 and 10, for those are the ones you will be using specifically with the children.
- Read the entire scripture passage aloud, slowly, at least two times. *Read it the first time* as if you had never heard it before. Picture in your mind the people who might have heard this for the first time. Knowing that many of the early followers were outcasts of society and of the Jewish culture/religion, try to feel what they might have felt the first time they heard these words read to them. Next, read it as the people in your congregation

might read it or hear it. How would their reception of these words be different from the reception by the people in the original setting? Why would these differences occur?
- Reflect on this passage; then write down any thoughts, questions, or ideas that you might have. *Do not neglect this step.*
- Which verses/verse do you think would be most appropriate for a Children's Sermon?

    I chose verse 9, particularly the following phrases: "you are ...a royal priesthood, ... God's own people, in order that you may proclaim the mighty acts of him who called you out of darkness into his marvelous light" and verse 10a, "Once you were not a people, but now you are God's people." You may decide to use another one.
- Offer the scripture as a prayer to God:

    *Thank you, God, for this Bible passage. It tells me how very special we are to you. Sometimes I need to hear that again to believe it. You know that I must believe your great love for me, in my heart and soul, before I can teach the children your great love for them. Give me wisdom and courage as I develop the Children's Sermon. All these things I ask in the name of your precious son, Jesus. Amen.*
- Spend a few minutes in silence, asking God to bless your work in preparation and to give you any thoughts that would be helpful to you during this time.

### D. Theme (s):

I shall use, in some manner, all of the themes I named earlier: Creation, God's Self-Revelation, People of God, and Faith-Response.

### E. Materials Needed
- Pictures of modern royalty (Queen Elizabeth II of England; Princess Diana; Prince Ranier and Princess Grace of Monaco; King Juan Carlos and Queen Sofia of Spain), each one on a half sheet of landscape cardstock. Put notes on the back of each one as to who he or she is/was. Try to choose pictures where the person is wearing royalty clothing, crown, medals, crest, etc.
- Bible
- Hand mirrors, preferably one for each child, but two or three could share. (Some of the dollar stores or large superstores

have inexpensive hand mirrors. The mirrors can come in useful for many different Children's Sermons).
- Handout card for each child

### F. Outline

- Invite the children forward and greet them as they sit around you.
- Read 1 Peter 2:9–10.
- Ask, "Did you hear me read that 'you are a royal priesthood?'"
- When we think of royalty, we think of kings, queens, princes, and princesses.
- Show pictures, one at a time, of Queen Elizabeth, Prince Rainer, Princess Grace, Princess Diana, King Juan Carlos, and Queen Sofia. Give a brief one- or two- sentence statement of who the person is or was (i.e., "Queen Elizabeth is the queen of England, and has been their queen for ___ years" or "Princess Diana became a princess because she married the Prince of Wales. She died in a car accident about __ years ago.") With each picture, ask the children, how they know that person is part of a royal family (crown, tiara, royal crest, medals, medallions, etc.). Mention that royal families have *responsibilities* to their people, things they must do to take care of and provide for them.
- Give each child or pair of children a hand mirror.
- Ask them to look at themselves as you continue asking them questions, "Do you see any crowns? Any medals? Any tiaras? Anything to show that you are part of the royalty?"
- Tell the children that they are indeed part of God's royal priesthood.
- What is the royal priesthood to do? ("Proclaim the mighty acts of him who called you out of darkness," or, simply put, "tell others about Jesus.") Remind them that they "belong to God's Family!"
- Closing words: "And the next time you begin to wonder *just who you are*, remember these words: "You are a royal priesthood!"
- Give children handouts and pray with them.

### G. Handout Suggestion

Summary phrase: "You are part of the royal family of God and Jesus Christ." Show picture of crowns, royalty, Jesus.

### H. Index Card

- Invite the children forward; greet them
- Read 1 Peter 2:9–10.
- Pics of royalty.
- Hand mirror exercise
- Closing words: "And the next time you begin to wonder *just who you are*, remember these words: "You are a royal priesthood!"
- Give children handouts and pray with them:

*Thank you, God,*
*for sending Jesus,*
*for choosing us to be*
*part of your family,*
*for giving us*
*an important job to do—*
*to tell others*
*about your Son Jesus.*
*In His name we pray. Amen.*

# Additional Ways to Include Children in the Worshiping Experience

### Children as Worship Leaders

Children can learn to provide leadership during the worship service.

I am aware of at least one congregation that once a month has the children (elementary grades) provide much of the leadership in the worship service, such as reading the scriptures, saying prayers, reading the offertory invitation, and helping to pass and collect the offering plates and communion trays.

The great advantage of including children in this way–beginning at an early age–is that they definitely feel more a part of the church. They begin to learn the roles and responsibilities of church membership long before they graduate from high school and go off on their own, many times to walk away from both church attendance and church responsibility.

The downside of this particular program was that the adult leaders for this program spent most of the other Sundays getting the children prepared for leading the service. I did not actually observe these preparations (just heard them described at length when I had been interviewed for a position), but I would hope that those other Sundays in the month involved more than just being a preparing ground for the children's one Sunday a month in leadership.

However, this program could be modified in some ways so that children were in leadership positions occasionally. Once a quarter, one or two children read scripture and say one or two of the prayers in the service. The main thing is to help prepare the children well. If they're saying a prayer, work with whoever is in charge of the worship service to find out what kinds of themes and hymns will be included in that day's service. Some suggestions for this are:

- If there is a given prayer, help the child work with pronunciation and enunciation.
- Make certain that the child can be seen by the congregation (you may need to have a stepstool for the shorter children).
- Practice with the child in the sanctuary or wherever you have your worship services.
- If there are microphones, let the child have a chance to practice using the microphone (this can confuse even adults who have never spoken into a microphone!).
- Go over their parts–one more time–the morning of the worship service.
- Enlist the help of the parents so that the child can also practice at home. (As a senior minister, I always go over my sermons two or three or more times before I preach on Sunday mornings. Good preparation makes all the difference.)
- Go through the same steps with children who will be reading scripture.

If the children are learning some songs in their Sunday school classes or Children's Worship/extended sessions, have them sing in the worship service every couple of months. This does not have to be a "grand performance" by any means. The children can be called forward during the Children's Sermon, along with the person who will be either playing an accompaniment (piano, guitar, etc.) or leading them, a capella, and they can sing their song(s) during the time in which you would have led them in the Children's Sermon.

### The Prayer Mentoring Ministry

Another very effective way for the children to become more involved with other church members is through a Prayer Mentoring Ministry.

A firm believer in the power of prayer, I struggled many years ago with ways to enhance prayer relationships in the congregation I was serving at the time. I knew how important and life-changing my own prayer life had been. After working with adults in starting a couple of prayer ministries, I realized that we needed to do something for the children. (I had already been teaching the children prayer habits and opportunities during my work with them in their Children's worship time every week.) It was time to begin a program where adults would begin a one-to-one partnership to pray for the babies, children, and youth in our congregation. I named this ministry the Prayer Mentoring Ministry. Listed below are the various parts of this ministry (and note that the youth are also included in this prayer ministry):

### List Babies, Children, and Youth

Make a list of all the non-adults in your church, including those who are frequent visitors in addition to member families. You will want to have their birth dates, name of parents/grandparents/guardians; and an address for mailing. You will need to do a lot of publicity for this ministry so that families of the children and other church members will know what it entails.

You will need two index cards for each baby, child, or youth. On each card write the name of the child, the birth date, the address, and adult relative(s). This can be done on a computer, using mailing labels (makes it much easier than writing two copies by hand). One of these cards will be given to the person who is going to be the prayer mentor; the other copy is kept in your files, with the name of that child's prayer mentor.

### Create a Chart

Now put all the names you listed in the step above and put them on a chart. If you have many children and youth, you can sort them by categories (i.e., babies, preschool, elementary grades, middle school, high school, even by specific grades). Beside each name leave a blank so that a church member can sign up to pray for that baby, child, or youth.

I usually also include a note at the bottom of each chart, in large print:

PARENTS and/or FRIENDS: If you notice that we have left out one of our babies, children, or youth, please contact me immediately. Thanks for your help with this.

### Explain Prayer Mentoring to Prospective Mentors

Prepare a list of what being a prayer mentor entails. Here is an example of such a list:

## Suggestions for Being a Prayer Mentor

1. Choose an index card from the basket outside the sanctuary. It will have the name, address, and possibly the phone number and/or birth date of a baby, child or teenager on it.
2. Find the name you drew on the charts of our babies, children, and youth (they will be listed in alphabetical order by last name); write your name on the blank line next to the name of your baby, child, or youth.
3. Put this list and the index card in a special place at home where you can find them easily.
4. Covenant with God to pray for your baby, child, or youth every week (more, if possible):
   - Pray that God will bless the child and family.
   - Pray that God will keep the child safe.
   - Pray that God will help the child to learn and to "grow in wisdom and in stature."
4. Send the person you're praying for a card, telling him or her that you will be praying weekly for him or her.
5. Look for the person in church so that you can introduce yourself. hello/
6. Send seasonal cards as you wish.
7. Please, no gifts or outings together. This is a prayer ministry, and it is not meant to be a forum for developing a relationship with the child or teen. If the family invites you to something, that is fine, but it is NOT appropriate for you to get together one-on-one with the person you're praying for.

Thank you for your support and your prayers in this prayer mentoring ministry for our children and youth. Be assured that you WILL make a difference.

**Questions? Contact** (your name)

One copy of this list would be poster size so that people could read it at a glance. Another copy would be a half-page (landscape) size, with enough copies for each person who wishes to be a part of the prayer mentoring ministry. Each person who signs up to be a prayer mentor would take one of these smaller copies with them as a reminder of what they are to do.

I find it helpful to insert a generic picture of a child from one of my computer art programs, for an attention-getter, on both the large poster and the individual handouts.

### Set up a Display Table

You will need the following items:

- the poster with "Suggestions for Being a Prayer Mentor"
- the handouts with "Suggestions for Being a Prayer Mentor"
- a basket with the index cards you have prepared with names and vital information of the babies, children, and youth
- the chart for signing up
- pencils and/or pens
- someone to sit or stand at the table to answer questions and help with the process

I have found it helpful to advertise this ministry in several ways: announcements before the worship service; newsletter articles; bulletin inserts; word-of-mouth through various groups in the church.

You will need to use some of the above resources to continue encouraging your mentors during the coming months, reminding them of special times to remember their mentorees.

# Recommended Books

## Suggested Children's Books

Alexander, Pat. *My First Bible: Wonderful Stories for Young Children.* Intercourse, Penn.: Good Books, 1997. I seldom use this for reading aloud to the children. However, the pictures are very colorful, and often I'll show a picture or two to illustrate the story we are using as the basis for the Children's Sermon. Sometimes I even tell the story, in simple terms, holding the book so that the children can see the pictures.

Beers, V. Gilbert. *The Toddler's Bible.* Colorado Springs: Cook Communications Ministries, 1992. (See notes from above; I use this book in a similar fashion; between the two, I find many pictures for illustration of Bible stories I want to tell the children.)

Brokering, Herbert F. (hymnist). *Earth & All Stars.* Malaysia: Morehouse Publishing, 2002.

Carwell, L'Ann. *God Gives New Life.* St. Louis: Concordia Publishing House, 1981.

dePaola, Tomie. *The Parables of Jesus.* New York: Holiday House, 1987.

Greene, Rhonda Gowler. *The Beautiful World That God Made.* Grand Rapids, Mich.: Eerdmans Books for Young Readers, 2002.

Hoffman, Mary, and Jackie Morris. *Miracles: Wonders Jesus Worked.* New York: Penguin Books for Young Readers, 2001.

Hudson, Wade. *God Smiles When.* Nashville: Abingdon Press, 2002.

Jeffs, Stephanie. *If You'd Been There in Bible Times.* Nashville: Abingdon Press, 2000.

McBratney, Sam. *I'm Sorry.* Hong Kong. HarperCollins, 2000.

Munsch, Robert. *Love You Forever.* Willowdale, Ontario, Canada: A Firefly Book, 1995.

Phifer, Martha Nelson. *The Colors of Christmas.* Scottdale, Penn.: Herald Press, 1995.

Rock, Lois, and Louise Rawlings. *Sad News, Glad News; Easter-time Prayers for Little Children.* Colorado Springs: A Lion Book, 1997.

Rosen, Michael J. *The Greatest Table: A Banquet to Fight against Hunger.* New York: Harcourt Brace & Company, 1994.

Sasso, Sandy Eisenberg. *God's Paintbrush.* Woodstock, Vt.: Jewish Lights Publishing, 1992.

Tudor, Tasha (illus). *And It Was So: Words from Scripture.* Philadelphia: The Westminster Press, 1988.

## Suggested Resource Books

Cavalletti, Sofia. *The Religious Potential of the Child.* New York: Paulist Press, 1973. A classic in this field, Cavaletti's grasp of what matters in working with children in the religious setting is excellent. Her long experience with children definitely shines through as she describes the basics of the Christian faith and how each relates to the child, and the child to them.

Cully, Iris V. *Education for Spiritual Growth.* San Francisco: Harper and Row, 1984. This is still the classic study, by a noted authority on religious education, that shows how the spiritual life can be nurtured at each age level, both in the classroom/ Sunday school/Children's worship, and through individual study. Cully explores in depth the quest for serenity and the process of spiritual development. This book draws upon a variety of biblical, theological, and psychological resources.

Daley-Harris, Shannon. *Providing What God Requires and Children Need: Justice, Kindness, and Faith.* Washington, D.C.: Children's Defense Fund, 2003. The goal of the Children's Defense Fund is to provide a strong, effective voice for all the children of America who cannot vote, lobby, or speak for themselves. It includes worship, education, community outreach, and advocacy resources for Protestant, Catholic, Episcopal, Jewish, and other faith traditions.

Davidson, Linda N. (Ed). *Creative Ideas for Advent (Vol. 2).* Prescott, Ariz.: Educational Ministries, Inc., 1990. This book is exactly what its title suggests—many creative ways of introducing children to the Advent season. It contains stories, plays, crafts, pictures, worship resources, and many other things. It can be used effectively as a "brainstorm center" when you are pondering what to do with the Children's Sermon on a particular Sunday in Advent.

Dingwall, Cindy. *Bible Time with Kids: 400 Bible-based Activities to Use with Children.* Nashville: Abingdon Press, 1997.

_____. *Bible Verse Fun with Kids: 200• Ideas and Activities That Help Children Learn and Live Scripture.* Nashville: Abingdon Press, 2004. Both of the Dingwall books have many ideas and activities that could be a source of creative thinking on your part. Both are based on scripture verses (and you will find a listing of the verses in both of these books), so these could be very helpful if you get stuck on one of those "child-unfriendly" verses some Sunday.

Drushal, Mary Ellen. *On Tablets of Human Hearts: Christian Education with Children.* Grand Rapids, Mich.: Zondervan, 1991. Another classic, this book is a good reminder of how children learn and how their learning styles should affect our teaching.

Frank, Marjorie. *I Can Make a Rainbow: Things to Create and Do for Children and Their Grown-up Friends.* Nashville: Incentive Publications, 1976. This is a marvelous book that contains hundreds of creative ideas, all categorized by different media, such as pencil/pen/crayon/chalk, paper, paint, cloth/yarn/string.

Halverson, Delia. *How Do Our Children Grow? Introducing Children to God, Jesus, the Bible, Prayer, and Church.* Rev. ed. St. Louis: Chalice Press, 1999. This book is a must for all those who work with children in the church. I find it helpful to go back and reread parts of this book every so often.

_____. *Teaching and Celebrating the Christian Seasons: A Guide for Pastors, Teachers, and Worship Leaders.* St. Louis: Chalice Press, 2003.

_____. *What's in Worship?.* St. Louis: Chalice Press, 2009.

Hanson, Richard Simon. *Worshiping with the Child.* Nashville: Abingdon Press, 1988. Hanson includes some helpful information about ways to include children in the worshiping community.

Lingo, Susan L. *Peace Makers: 13 Fun Filled Bible Lessons about Peace.* Cincinnati: Standard Publishing Company, 2001. Although this book is written to be used as a thirteen–week curriculum teaching about peace and peacemaking, it also can be used as a "think tank" if you want to emphasize the topic of peace in your Children's Sermon. Some very unique ideas are included in this book.

McGinnis, Kathleen, and Barbara Oehlberg. *Starting Out Right: Nurturing Young Children as Peacemakers.* Oak Park, Ill.: Meyer Stone Books, 1988. This book gives some of the theology and theory behind peacemaking, including how children process violence, develop racial attitudes, grow in their understanding of older people, and develop a respect for the earth. There is much to learn in this classic.

Riley, Kelly. *Celebrate Easter.* Carthage, Ill.: Shining Star, 1987. This book can be helpful as you plan for Easter and the Sundays leading up to and following it.

Roehlkepartain, Jolene L. *Teaching Kids to Care & Share: 300+ Mission & Service Ideas for Children.* Nashville: Abingdon Press, 2000. Filled with more than 300 inventive, hands-on ideas and activities that involve children in service to one another, their churches, and local communities and the world, this book would be helpful if you're going to talk with the children about serving others.

Scheilhing, Theresa O'Callaghan. *Our Treasured Heritage: Teaching Christian Meditation to Children.* New York: Crossroad, 1981. Again, this is a "one of its kind,:" classic resource. Written especially to help parents teach meditation to children, it also has some very good tips for those persons in our churches who work with children and who develop and lead the children's sermon.

Thomas, Denis. *The Face of Christ.* Garden City, N.Y.: Doubleday, 1979. In addition to being a commentary on Christian art with particular emphasis on the face of Christ, this art volume shows paintings from the early catacombs, the Middle Ages, the Renaissance, and into modern times. A valuable resource to have for the occasional Children's Sermon.

Weber, Hans-Ruedi. *Immanuel: The Coming of Jesus in Art and the Bible.* Grand Rapids, Mich: Eerdmans, 1984. This art book has some wonderful pictures of the life of Christ, including many that could be used for Advent.

# Scriptures Used

| CHAPTER | TITLE | SCRIPTURE |
|---|---|---|
| 1 | Why a Children's Sermon? | Ma. 18:1–5; Deut. 6:5–9; Heb. 8:10–11; Mt. 18:6 |
| 2 | How Well Do You Know Your Audience? | 1 Cor. 9:19–23 |
| 3 | How Do You Craft the Children's Sermon? | Mt. 13:45–46; Is. 2:2–3 |
| 4 | What about the People in the Pews? | Mk. 4:30–32 |
| 5 | What Are the Vital Tools for the Journey? | Deut. 6:4–9 |
| 6 | What Are Some Helpful Insights for the Journey? | Lk. 9:1–6; 1 Tim. 4:11–16; Ex. 18:13–23 |
| 7 | Year B/Advent 1 | Is. 64:1–9; Ps. 80:1–7, 17–19; Mark 13:24–37; 1 Cor. 1:3–9 |
| | Year B/Advent 2 | Is. 40:1–11; Ps 85:1–2, 8–13; 2 Pet. 3:8–15a; Mk. 1:1–8a |
| | Year B/Epiphany 2 | 1 Sam. 3:1–10; Ps. 139: 1–6, 13–18; 1 Cor. 6:12–20; Jn. 1:43–51 |
| | Year B/Lent 1 | Gen. 9:8–17; Ps. 25:1–10; 1 Peter 3:18–22; Mk. 1:9–15 |
| | Year B/Lent 3 | Ex. 20:1–17; Ps. 19; 1 Cor. 1:18–25; Jn. 2:13–22 |
| | Year B/Palm Sunday | Ps. 118:1–2, 19–29; Mk. 11:1–11; Jn. 12:12–16 |

| CHAPTER | TITLE | SCRIPTURE |
|---------|-------|-----------|
| 8 | Year C/Lent 5 | Is. 43:16–21; Ps. 126; Ps. 119:9–16; Phil. 3:4b–14; Jn. 12:1–8 |
| | Year C/Easter 2 | Acts 5:27–32; Ps. 150; Rev. 1:4–8; Jn. 20:19–31 |
| | Year C/Easter 4 | Acts 9:36–43; Ps. 23; Rev. 7:9–17; Jn. 10:22–30 |
| | Year C/Easter 6 | Acts 16:9–15; Ps. 67; Rev. 21:10, 22–22:5; Jn. 14:23–29; Jn. 5:1–9 |
| | Year C/Proper 5 | 1 Kings 17:8–16; Ps. 146; Gal. 1:11–24; Lk. 7:11–17 |
| | Year C/Proper 19 | Jer. 4:11–12, 22–28; Ps. 14; 1 Tim. 1:12–17; Lk. 15:1–10 |
| 9 | Year A/Advent 3 | Is. 35:1–10; Ps. 146:5–10; Jas. 5:7–10; Mt. 11:2–11; Lk. 1:46–55 |
| | Year A/Epiphany | Is. 60:1–6; Ps. 72:1–7, 10–14; Eph. 3:1–12; Mt. 2:1–12 |
| | Year A/Lent 1 | Gen.2:15–17; 3:1–7; Ps. 32; Rom. 5:12–19; Mt. 4:1–11 |
| | Year A/Lent 3 | Ex. 17:1–7; Ps. 95; Rom. 5:1–11; Jn. 4:5–42 |
| | Year A/Easter | Ps. 118:1–2, 14–24; Jer. 31:1–6; Col. 3:1–4; Mt. 28:1–10 |
| | Year A/Easter 5 | Acts 7:55–60; Ps. 31:1–5, 15–16; 1 Pet. 2:2–10; Jn. 14:1–14 |
| | | |